MOM JOKES

Like Dad Jokes, Only Smarter

Lisa Beth Johnson
Phoebe Bottoms

PORTABLE
PRESS
San Diego, California

Portable Press
An imprint of Printers Row Publishing Group
10350 Barnes Canyon Road, Suite 100, San Diego, CA 92121
www.portablepress.com • mail@portablepress.com

Printers Row Publishing Group is a division of Readerlink Distribution Services, LLC.
Portable Press is a registered trademark of Readerlink Distribution Services, LLC.

Correspondence regarding the content of this book should be sent to Portable
Press, Editorial Department, at the above address.

Publisher: Peter Norton
Associate Publisher: Ana Parker
Art Director: Charles McStravick
Senior Developmental Editor: April Graham Farr
Cover Designer: Rosemary Rae
Production Team: Julie Greene, Rusty von Dyl
Designer: Susan Engbring

Cover image: bortonia/Digital Vision Vectors via Getty Images

Library of Congress Control Number: 2020946252
ISBN: 978-1-68412-952-2

Printed in the United States of America

25 24 23 22 21   1 2 3 4 5

Q: What's the quickest way to spread gossip?

A: Post it online, call your neighbor, or tell a toddler who has just learned to talk.

· · · · ·

My eight-year-old son would make
a great parole officer someday.
He never lets anyone finish a sentence.

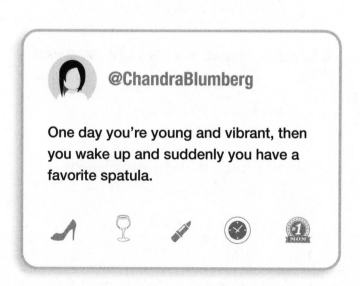

@ChandraBlumberg

One day you're young and vibrant, then you wake up and suddenly you have a favorite spatula.

Mom's favorite word: Yes.

Mom's two favorite words:
You're right.

Mom's three favorite words:
Love you, Mommy.

Mom's four favorite words:
I did it myself.

Mom's five favorite words:
I wanna take a nap.

Mom's least favorite word: No.

Mom's least two favorite words:
Watch me.

Mom's three least favorite words:
I want that!

Mom's four least favorite words:
But I'm not tiiiiiiiiired.

Mom's five least favorite words:
MOM MOM MOM MOM MOM.

I learned to cook from my mother...
I made a point of watching everything she did,
so I could do everything the opposite way.

. . . . .

If my daughter complains too much,
I make her sit in her room for an hour
listening to her super-realistic crying baby.

@not_thenanny

I just wanted five minutes to drink my
coffee, so I sent my kid in the other room
to look for a toy that's in my pocket.
Follow me for more parenting hacks.

When my daughter didn't accept my friend request,
it hurt my feelings. But then my mom
friend-requested me, and I suddenly understood.

· · · · ·

I'm putting my son through school single-handedly.
Well, I shoved him through the doorway while
holding a toddler, but it's a start.

· · · · ·

Being a mom means your kids
never expecting to hear "I'm sorry."

Last week I told my husband
that the last three words I want
to hear while I'm making love are,
"Honey, I'm home!" Ever since then,
he's been on time every day!

@Marlebean

Mom
Mom
Mommy
Mom
Ma
MOM
MOMMY
MOMMYMOMMYMOMMYMOMMY
MOMMYMOMMMMMMMMMMY
What are you eating?
Xanax.

Five-year-old son: I love you so much, I'd cry every day if I had a different mom.

Mom: Then what's your excuse for the last four years?

@domesticgoddss

Ever notice in the story of the 3 bears, Papa Bear's porridge is piping hot, baby's is perfect, & poor Mama Bear's is cold?
I get it now.

Sometimes I can't believe that I already
have a sixteen-year-old daughter.
Then I remember she's only twelve but
wearing a push-up bra.

. . . . .

It's important to offer your kids
a lot of choices for dinner,
such as "eat what I give you," or
"don't," or "go to your room,"
or "eat what I give you."

My husband is a stay-at-home dad.
I take the kids to school—he stays at home.
I pick them up and take them to soccer practice—
he stays at home.

· · · · ·

I let my six-year-old daughter paint my
toenails and it definitely looks like she thinks
I have hooves instead of feet.

· · · · ·

When I tucked him in tonight,
my kid asked me if I was happy.
I told him I was on cloud wine.

· · · · ·

Life is better with kids.
Both are better with wine.

Steps to Getting Your Kid to Brush Their Teeth

1. See if the brush is wet.

2. Smell their breath.

3. Get them an electric toothbrush with their favorite cartoon character on it to make brushing more fun.

4. Buy a decoy toothbrush with a camera in it and retire to your secret lair to wait and see if brushing takes place.

5. Once their teeth fall out from not brushing, make a necklace for them to wear for the rest of their lives.

If you asked me if I'd rather be rich, famous, or a good mom, I'd say two of those three would be nice. After all, it'd be no fun to be *poor* and famous.

· · · · ·

No week is a good week for your four-year-old to learn knock-knock jokes.

@Lurkathomemom

Mary Poppins voice
Ok, children! Time to go!
[15 min later]
Batman voice
I said let's go.

Being a mother is like being a superhero: everyone's a little bit scared of you, and you're always trying to keep a bunch of monsters from destroying everything.

None of my children will ever appreciate how much time I've spent planning every moment of their lives.

. . . . .

Renting a bounce house for my kid's birthday is pretty expensive, but can you really put a price on the happiness I feel being left alone?

. . . . .

Now that I'm a mother myself, I've realized my mom is my hero. And you know what they say: never meet your heroes.

You're a lot more chill and laid-back when you're an older mom. For instance, I just let my son run in a circle for two hours because I couldn't chase him anymore.

· · · · ·

They say being nice to other people's kids won't kill you— but honestly, I'd rather not risk it.

@patricksara

A baby shower game requested everyone write parenting advice on a notecard, so I wrote down my favorite margarita recipe.

I *love* being a single mom
and putting a positive spin
on everything that sucks!

. . . . .

The most magical day of my life
was when I became a mother.
A close second is the day
I became a mother whose
kid moved out of her house.

• • • • • • • • • • • • • • • •

A Poem to My Son

Roses are red
Violets are blue
Sugar is sweet
And so are
you know not to do that
at the dinner table!

• • • • • • • • • • • • • • •

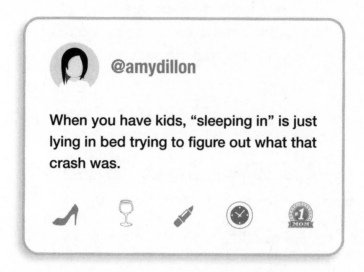

@amydillon

When you have kids, "sleeping in" is just lying in bed trying to figure out what that crash was.

I am at my most relaxed when I'm running around looking frazzled, because the second I stop and sit down, my kids will need something.

· · · · ·

As a mom, the scariest seconds you can have are the ones between absentmindedly licking a brown smudge off your finger and realizing it's just chocolate.

Being a working mom isn't that bad,
but I much prefer to be a mom who is
just sitting on the couch doing nothing
for a fricking second.

New Mom Email Template

Hi, _____!!!

So nice to hear from you. It has *indeed*
been a while! I've been doing pretty well
with my new, darling _____, whom
we've named _____. Things are good
what was that oops I didn't mean to type
that ha-ha _____ says the baby is crying
again so I've got to go let's definitely try
to get together soon ok/

Zp,

_____

@bourgeoisalien

"everything you're doing as a parent is wrong" the new parenting book by everyone on the internet

No matter how old he gets,
my son always calls me
once a month to remind me
to pay his phone bill.

· · · · ·

There will be times when it feels like you've
failed as a mom, but whatever you do,
don't ever run that feeling by your adult kids.

· · · · ·

I used to want it all:
a career, a husband, kids…
Now, do *you* want any of it?

We told our teen he was adopted.
He was surprised, but we're giving him
a couple of minutes to pack until his
new parents come get him.

. . . . .

Well, I guess I'll have to change the
"____ DAYS WITHOUT ANY CRYING
ABOUT VEGETABLES" sign back to 0!

 @maughamom

I don't care how cute your kid is. When
you wake up in the middle of the night
and see them standing next to your bed,
they are terrifying.

There's no way to be the perfect mother or create a perfect kid, unless you ask my mother-in-law about my husband.

. . . .

When you look at your mother, you're seeing pure love ... but if you look at your mother like that again, you're going to see a wrath hotter than a thousand suns.

. . . .

Mothers are like glue: you don't always notice them trying to hold it all together, and also why are they always so sticky?

. . . .

My granddaughter says a grandma is like having a manual for life, which explains why she only half listens to my instructions and then ends up with a screw loose.

Stranger in line next to me at the grocery store: Being a mom is the most rewarding job there is, because you get paid in love!

Me: Yeah … Do you know if they accept love here, or should I just charge it?

. . . . .

Don't tell me not to cry over spilled milk unless *you've* also just knocked the contents of your breast pump onto the floor.

Being a mom is about opposites: strength and softness, love and discipline, spinach and cookies, crazed laughter and shower crying … sometimes all in one day!

@Housewifeofhell

What's it called when you're anxious enough to be a Helicopter Mom, but really, really lazy? A Blimp Mom? Yeah, I'm that.

I gave my kids life, but they gave me a great excuse to cancel plans with crappy friends ... so I think we're even.

· · · · ·

Be the mom you want them to remember, because someday they might have to decide whether you can live with them or not.

• • • • • • • • • • • •

What to Say
If Your Teen Comes Home
with a Hickey

"That better be a smudge from some
junk food I don't let you eat."

"Just tell me the other person is your age
and I'll look the other way."

"Didn't I buy you, like, three turtlenecks
last winter? Next time, at least try."

"It's cool, but your dad gave me a
better one yesterday."

• • • • • • • • • • • •

Q: What do a rope and a toddler have in common?

A: They're always "knotty."

. . . . .

Imagine the shock on my kids' faces the first time I explain that their father is also fully capable of making them a snack.

. . . . .

My child recently offered me some parental advice, which was nice, because I was worried ten might be too young to start charging him rent.

. . . . .

It's sad when your kids get too big to put on your shoulders so you can pretend you're a khaleesi with a baby dragon.

@Donna_McCoy

I wish I had the optimism of a mom who puts fresh fruit into lunch boxes every morning.

When her last kid moved out of the house, my mom got a new cat. When my last kid moves out, I'm getting a new phone number.

· · · · ·

It's cruel when beauty companies try to sell eye cream to tired moms … I'd have to sleep longer than I've been alive to reverse *this* damage.

Knock-knock. Who's there?
Well, actually I don't care.
Could you please just hold my baby
while I take a one-minute shower?

. . . . .

I wish I loved anything as much as
my husband loves to ask if I need
anything and then immediately fall
asleep on the couch.

. . . . .

Sometimes you get so mad at your child
the only thing that helps is to daydream
about how mad you're going to be when
they get their first tattoo.

. . . . .

My kid caught me practicing my withering
stare in the bathroom mirror. Now I'm
terrified I've lost the upper hand.

If you've spent more than a thousand hours deleting pictures of extreme face close-ups from your phone … you might be a parent.

I'm trying to find a nice way to say that next Mother's Day, I don't want to see, hear, touch, or smell anyone I married or gave birth to.

Seven species of animal have moms who eat their young. After my kid's last meltdown at the grocery store, it almost became eight.

. . . . .

I have to do the grocery shopping in my house, because the last time one of my husbands went out for a pack of something he never came back.

I just know that on my deathbed,
my son is going to lean over me
and gently whisper,
"Mom, can I have a snack?"

. . . . .

I know a mom who has the time
to make her own soap …
I don't even have time to *use* soap.

 @mommyshorts

Asked to switch seats on the plane because I was sitting next to a crying baby. Apparently, that's not allowed if the baby is yours.

MOM MONTHS

....

JANUARY: Starts with your kids throwing a fit if they don't get to stay up many hours past their bedtime. Ends 112 days later. God help you if it snows.

FEBRUARY: Be your kid's Valentine, celebrate Black History Month and Presidents' Day, learn what the weather's going to do from a rodent, and you're out.

MARCH: Daylight savings *and* Saint Patrick's Day? If your kids aren't crying about the time change, they're crying because you didn't dress them in green. Good luck!

APRIL: Begins with a day of pranks. Showers bring flowers and so ... much ... mud. Hope your kids aren't as afraid of the Easter bunny as you are of doing your taxes!

MAY: Between Cinco de Mayo and Mother's Day, you can justify a daily margarita for the first half of the month. Otherwise, just enjoy the weather!

JUNE: School's out and now it's your turn to entertain them every hour of the day. Father's Day is somewhere in there, I guess. It's not important.

JULY: All you can do is close your eyes, cross your fingers, and hope your kid doesn't lose one in a firecracker accident. Also, it's probably very hot.

AUGUST: If it wasn't hot before, it certainly is now. Maybe someone has a pool. Anyone. Who can you bribe to let your kid swim at their pool!?

SEPTEMBER: It's cooled down and now you can think. The kids are probably back in school and there's Labor Day: a holiday that's not about labor.

OCTOBER: Better hope you bought your kids' costumes eight months ago, because they all want to be some obscure character you won't find in any store!

NOVEMBER: Holiday season has arrived—time for Mom to yoke herself to the oven and cook for the entire extended family, who only sort of appreciates it.

DECEMBER: The most wonderful time of the year has finally arrived … the time when moms get an excuse to shop as much as they want (though not for themselves).

@katewhinehall

My 4yo just shut the bathroom door on me while I was inside and told me I was in jail. So, I locked the door. I love this game.

It's not so much that I need a glass of *wine* at the end of the day, as much as I just need to ingest something my kid won't insist on having some of.

· · · · ·

Sometimes I can blow my kid's mind by answering her question with, "What if I were to tell you ... that I already told you the last time you asked!"

My teenager just informed me that parental-advisory warnings are mostly for parents, and he's not exactly wrong.

· · · · ·

TGIF! *The weekend is here!* Oh, wait. I almost forgot. I'm a mom.

· · · · ·

It takes all of my self-control not to scream, "Nooooo!" when my kids ask if they can help me with anything.

What do I want for my birthday this year, Sweetie? Nothing, really. Maybe just a day to spend warning my twenty-year-old self.

31

All the buckles and straps on this car seat are good practice for the ones on the straitjacket it's going to put me in.

· · · · ·

My kid asked for a bird. I told him if he wants something that just whistles and shrieks all day, he can go live at my mother-in-law's house.

@workingmom86

"Will I ever live in a clean house again?"
*shakes magic 8 ball
*magic 8 ball explodes and makes a mess

My sister, handing me my crying child: Being an aunt is better than being a mom because I can just give them back to you.

Me: You get custody of them if anything *happens* to us ... and it would be a *real shame* if something happened to us, wouldn't it?

· · · · · ·

My friend suggested I read *Fifty Shades of Grey*. I told her if I wanted to get off on being tortured, I'd just go to more PTA meetings.

· · · · · ·

Family-road-trip hack: the first time your kids ask if you're there yet, just say yes and drop them off wherever you happen to be.

Rock Star Demands:

**Van Halen: M&M's
(but no brown ones)**

**Axl Rose: square-shaped melon
(grown only in Japan)**

Eminem: eight Lunchables

Joe Jonas: twelve puppies

My Kid's Demands:

**Grilled cheese, cut only in
"silly" slices**

**Microwaved chicken potpie, with
the peas individually taken out**

**Strawberries
(no seeds)**

Thirteen puppies

@foxywinepocket

Son: Are you eating pie for breakfast?
Me (eating pie): No. Fruit casserole.
Want some?
Son: NO. I hate casserole.
Me (whispers): I know…

The only S&M I need are
"sangria" and "margaritas."

· · · · ·

My friend was complaining about
her son getting married …
My son is three, so the only
"wedding" I'm complaining about
is the bed kind.

@snarkymom

I feel like I'd be a much better parent if I didn't have to do it every day.

My kid asked me to tell him
a scary bedtime story,
so I told him about the twenty hours
of labor I suffered through.

· · · · ·

If my children ask me to read them
One Fish, Two Fish, Red Fish, Blue Fish
one more time, I'm going to
write a new book called
One Kid, Two Kid, I Want a New Kid.

Before my kids were born, I went on
vacation to Europe. Now that I'm a mom,
my only vacation is the occasional
solo trip to the bathroom.

. . . . .

Sometimes it's fun to get dressed up—
which mostly means putting on pants
that don't have elastic on them.

. . . . .

Some people send their kids to
educational day camps during
summer vacation. My son
learned that an egg explodes
if you put it in the microwave.
So, that's pretty much the same thing.

. . . . .

I used to try to stop my daughter
from crying about how unfair life is,
but then realized how much money
she could make as a soap-opera actress.
And I want a comfy retirement.

People say when you have kids you stop doing
what you love—but not me. I've always loved
hunting for cereal in car seats and scraping
dried ketchup off dirty plates!

. . . . .

"Thanks, but I already ate" is a
fun thing to say to someone who
is trying to hand you a baby.

. . . . .

My mom used to say that only boring
people are bored ... or something like that.
Anyway, I usually stopped listening
after the third word.

. . . . .

I overheard two older women talking about
how marriage has changed over the years.
One said, "I didn't sleep with my husband
until our wedding night. Did you?" The other
one said, "Maybe ... what's his name?"

I expected my best friend to cry
when I told her I was pregnant.
I didn't expect it to be over her finally
getting to be the skinny one.

. . . . .

I believe it was Tolstoy who said "Happy families
are all alike, but every unhappy family has a
mother that could really use a spa day."

@copymama

My 6yo carried our Google Home
Mini around the house all day asking
it question after question to the point
where I found it locked in the bathroom
crying with a glass of wine.

Can you be a good mom and also
root for the Grinch?

· · · · ·

Purgatory is a family car trip where
everyone's looking at their phones.
Hell is what happens when you take
the phones away.

 @momjeansplease

Last night at dinner, my son told me
I was pretty completely unprompted.
This morning at breakfast my daughter
called me a poop stain... completely
unprompted.
You win some you lose some, I guess.

PMS
stands for:

Puffy Midsection

Powerful Mood Swings

Please Make Sugar

Psychotic Monthly Snap

**Probably Murdered
Someone**

Pardon My Sobbing

@lastunicorn

Me: Hey kid what do you want for dinner?
8: Do you have cheese?
Me: yes
8: Do you have ham?
Me: yes
8: Do you have bread and mayo?
Me: YES
8: I want spaghetti

Time is an interesting thing … as my kid went from thirteen to nineteen, I aged fifty years.

. . . . .

People ask me how I keep my house so clean. It's easy: I made my kids go live in the yard.

My mother asked me to play FMK
and it took ten minutes before I
realized she thought that meant
"Family, Marriage, or Kids."

. . . .

Roses are red,
Violets are blue.
My toddler won't poop
Unless I do too.

. . . .

My stay-at-home husband has
been telling our kids that MOM
stands for "Made of Money."
I'm going to tell them DAD stands
for "Doesn't Add Dollars."

Q: What's the salary for a stay-at-home mom?
A: MiniMOM wage.

. . . . .

It's good to have kids, so you have someone
to take care of you when you're old.
Unfortunately, that's also why you have
to be nice to them.

. . . .

**I love exercising because
it's the only time I get
to pick up something heavy
that *isn't* screaming.**

. . . .

My husband's monthly poker games
have become much more intense
since we decided the loser also
has to be our kid's godparent.

Our house is full of teenagers, so there's constant crying and yelling, "You don't get me!" and threatening to leave the family. And you should see how my *kids* act!

· · · · ·

I'm a glass-half-full kind of person. I'm also a glass-half-empty person. Honestly, as long as it's a full-bodied red, I don't really care.

· · · · ·

I was watching TV with my children, having a glass of wine, and said, "You know, I love you more than life itself." They rolled their eyes and groaned, "Mom, that's obviously the wine talking." I said, "Oh, no, that's me talking to the wine."

· · · · ·

My husband kept going onto my Netflix account and screwing up my algorithm. So I locked him out of it by changing the password to the date of our wedding anniversary.

DATE NIGHT IDEAS

1. Re-create the night you conceived your child and reverse the curse.

2. Drop kids off at your parents', spend rest of the evening arguing about said kids.

3. Go to the concert of a band you hazily remember being good from the last time you got to listen to adult music.

4. Go to the movies and sleep.

5. Have a meal at a nice restaurant, ordering things you know your kids would hate. Bring home leftovers.

6. Enjoy a meal where no one gets sticky.

@good_one_rick

If you don't have a favorite stall in the local Target bathroom are you even a mom?

My husband and I made a rule to never go to bed angry. Who knew you could go six days without sleep?

. . . . .

I have a bucket list just like anyone else, but mine is filled with ice and a bottle of rosé, and has a sticky note on it that says "DRINK!"

47

If something happened to my husband, I could never remarry. Once was enough, thank you.

Kid: I got stung by a bee at school!

Mom: You should've gotten stung by an A!

· · · · ·

When I see two names carved on a tree, I don't think it's sweet. I think it's weird how many people bring a knife on a first date.

· · · · ·

My son is upset because his friends found out he was lying about having a girlfriend ... it's going to be worse once I tell him his friends are imaginary, too.

To get my toddler to eat I say, "Here comes the choo-choo!" It works because he knows he has to take a bite before I'll untie him from the tracks.

. . . . .

My three-year-old was taking a bath and pointed to his wiener and asked, "Is this my brain?" I said, "No, not yet."

 @crazyexhaustion

Me to baby: Say Dada!
Husband: You don't want her first word to be Mama?
Me: Hell no! The other 2 won't leave me alone. This one's yours.

I told my husband the kids weren't
eating their sandwiches and he
told me to just throw them out.
That seems a bit harsh.

. . . . .

Back in my day, we had to Uberpool
to school *both ways.*

. . . . .

If I'm feeling nice, I let my kids lick the batter
off the mixer. If I'm feeling extra nice,
I turn it off first.

. . . . .

My husband asked if I could
come to the phone. I said,
"Maybe ... if it's on vibrate."

FIRST KID VS THIRD KID

First kid: All-natural cleaning supplies.
Third kid: Industrial-strength bleach.

First kid: New outfit for the first day of school.
Third kid: "Just put on your brother's Halloween costume, you're going to miss the bus!"

First kid: No sugar, no processed foods, no artificial flavors.
Third kid: Popsicles are fruit.

First kid: Immediately take them to the ER if they cough once.
Third kid: "It'll probably grow back."

First kid: No screens, just classical music.
Third kid: Their iPad could sign a permission slip as their "legal guardian."

First kid: Spend months setting up their room to be the nicest one in the house.
Third kid: "Do you still live here? I thought you moved out ... I could really use that room for storage ..."

@carbosly

My husband brought the kids to a
baseball game, so I woke them up at 2am
to feed them candy.
No way I'm losing the "favorite parent"
battle.

I got my tubes tied because I didn't want kids ...
but when I got home, the kids were still there.

• • • • •

My husband thinks he's good at intimidating
our daughter's boyfriends, but all *I* have to do
is remind them I could be their mother-in-law.

• • • • •

I don't call it birth control ...
I call it "baby proofing my womb."

My mother-in-law expects me to treat my
husband the same way she did ...
so I guess I'll nag him until he moves out?

. . . . .

I'd rather tell my kids Santa doesn't exist
than tell them the "Elf on the shelf" isn't
really watching them.

They say diamonds
are a girl's best friend—
but for moms,
they're more of an
acquaintance.

A toddler gets more done when you turn your back for thirty seconds than most people get done in an entire week.

. . . . .

I finally got to go to the gym today, but I spent most of my time following people around and wiping down everything they touched.

. . . . .

I hope my kids look back someday and remember all of the couple of times I didn't yell at them.

When you have a kid, a husband,
and a dog, you never have to
cop to any of your own farts.

· · · · ·

My twelve-year-old and sixteen-year-old
are my sun and my moon, in that one
has prematurely aged me, and I only
see the other one at night.

 @midgardmomma

Parenthood is:
Telling your kids they can't eat
brownies for breakfast, then eating
brownies for breakfast after they
leave for school.

Bedtime Itinerary

7:25: "Time to get ready for bed!"

7:30: Brush teeth (suck on a dry toothbrush and fall off a stool three times).

7:33: Pee before bed. Or they disconnect their brain from their bladder and sit there kicking their feet.

7:38: Get in an argument about the pajamas you pick. Give in and let them pick pajamas. They choose a flower girl dress. Fine.

7:40: Book time. Get into a negotiation about how many books that takes so long, you could have read them five books.

7:50: "I forgot one thing I can't describe in a place that may or may not exist."

8:00: Lights out … you wish. Instead they're yelling at you for something that happened two days ago.

8:07: "I'm thirsty." Get them water and watch them drink an entire glass while a voice screams in the back of your head, "No, dummy! They didn't pee before bed, remember?"

8:10: Spend what seems to be the rest of your life adjusting the light in the room just right.

8:15: Close the door. Listen to them talk to themselves about nothing for half an hour.

@manda_like_wine

Added some honesty to the celebration by telling my kids that Father's Day is actually a celebration of me for making their father a father.

Whenever my dog goes for his water bowl, I go for my wineglass. That way neither of us is drinking alone.

· · · · ·

Every Mother's Day my children make me breakfast in bed. Good thing I taught them how to make bottomless mimosas.

· · · · ·

My son has his father's nose and my hair, and we both really need him to let go of them.

Your kid can do no wrong? Good for you.
I think there's only one more wrong thing
my kids *haven't* done.

@mommy_cusses

Your child's favorite toy is whichever one
they just lost.

I'm so sorry I was late for book club.
I was definitely *not* driving around the
neighborhood for an hour in my car
trying desperately to finish
the audiobook at double speed.

I recently discovered a great
relaxation technique that involves
watching videos of cats and dogs
getting along.

. . . .

**Cook a man a fish and you feed him
for an hour. Teach a man to fish
and you can get rid of him
for an entire weekend.**

. . . .

Stop saying I'm hard to shop for ...
the last time you went to
the store to get me tampons,
I was *very* appreciative!

. . . . . .

Someday I'll get old and
might not be able to hear my
children's voices. I only wish
that would happen right now.

@abhorrent_wife

looks up from phone
"Kids!! we're leaving the playground in 22 percent."

My kids say I have a short temper, but I don't think they'd like it if my temper lasted any longer.

· · · · ·

Please, lady at the park, tell me more about how I should raise my kids. I'm trying to join a gang, but I have to beat someone up as an initiation and I'd like it to be you.

· · · · ·

My kids and my garbage disposal eat only the *best* organic produce!

Mom 1: My son's perfect.

Mom 2: Does he look at his phone all day?

Mom 1: Nope.

Mom 2: Does he take your car without asking?

Mom 1: No, he doesn't.

Mom 2: Does he ever come home late?

Mom 1: Never.

Mom 2: I guess you really do have the perfect son. How old is he?

Mom 1: He'll be six months on Wednesday.

MY THREE-YEAR-OLD'S FAVORITE TOYS

- A lemon with a Band-Aid on it

- A zip tie found in the street

- Crayons and the nicest books in the house

- A flushing toilet

- The stall door in a public bathroom

- The most dangerous thing within five feet

- A kind of bug I've never seen before

- The dog's gross chew toy

- The litter box

- Anything attached to my face

I recently went to a wedding where you couldn't bring your kids *and* they didn't serve alcohol. Isn't that one of the circles of hell?

· · · · ·

I wish I were as good at reacting to our kids as my husband is. Whenever they start to misbehave, he immediately finds something to go do in the garage.

· · · · ·

You know you have teenagers when you find yourself worrying about where they are when you're standing right next to them.

· · · · ·

I have one smart kid: the one who always offers to set the table because she knows it's easier than doing the dishes afterward.

My mother-in-law is really cool to me.
Wait, I meant "cold."

· · · · ·

If your kids ask for a pet, glue some googly eyes
onto the bathtub hair catcher and tell them
it's a gerbil.

@mummacrazy

If you mean getting my 3yo to change
out of her Elsa dress into regular clothes
every day, then yes, I do participate in
extreme sports.

Q: What did one bottle of wine say to the other?

A: Chardon-*moi*, but haven't we met somewhere before?

. . . . .

My daughter thinks that an OB-GYN is where we get frozen yogurt.

. . . . .

There was a kid at the store whining for five minutes that he wanted a hamburger, and it made me really, really hungry for my birth control.

. . . . .

What's harder to imagine: the age of our universe, or my kid cleaning his room?

One of the biggest signs your teen is keeping something from you is that they're between the ages of thirteen and nineteen.

. . . . .

My five-year-old is a little too sassy for someone who puts her pants on backward most of the time.

. . . . .

The good thing about going back to work after having kids is that you have your mom-boss voice *perfected*.

My teen's "phone plan" is to never, ever put her phone down.

Motherhood Fantasy v. Motherhood Reality

Fantasy: I'm going to use only cloth diapers!
Reality: Give me whatever contains the most fluid-absorbing mystery gel.

Fantasy: I'm going to take the kids to Europe and let them see the world!
Reality: *googles hotels with pools within a five-mile radius*

Fantasy: I'm going to volunteer at school more than any other parent.
Reality: I couldn't tell you where their classroom is if my life depended on it.

Fantasy: I'm going to listen to everything they ever have to tell me.
Reality: I haven't heard a single word they've said in four years.

Fantasy: I'm never going to yell at my kids.
Reality: I *don't* yell at my kids. I just flip them off behind their backs.

@elizabethesther

I feel like 90% of parenting is just figuring out how much coffee I'm gonna need today.

I let my kids have one glass of champagne on New Year's Eve, but I give it to them in a Styrofoam cup that I poked a bunch of holes in.

· · · · ·

A recent study showed that women who are slightly overweight live longer than the husbands who point it out to them.

I love traveling, but it would be nice if
airlines treated their passengers with as
much respect as I give my kid's dirty socks
when I move them from the floor to
the hamper.

· · · · ·

If your teenager is talking too much, try
replacing her lip gloss with a glue stick.

· · · · · · · · · · · · · · · · · · · ·

**To be happy with a man,
you have to be able to
read his mind.
To be happy with a woman,
stay the hell out of there.**

· · · · · · · · · · · · · · · · · · · ·

They say that time waits for no one,
so "time" must be a teenager.

It's been raining all week, and at this
point my kids are just standing near
the windows, watching and waiting.
I should really let them in.

. . . . .

Instead of telling dates that I'm divorced,
I tell them I just got out of a ten-year debate.

. . . . .

My mother gave my husband a card that said
"Get better soon!" He called her and said thanks,
but he's perfectly healthy. She said, "I know,
but I still think you could get better."

. . . . .

The last time I had PMS, I wrote a fifteen-page
letter to my family detailing all the things they
do wrong. I call it my *menstrafesto*.

My husband must have the dirtiest mind, because the entire time I've known him he's never changed anything in it.

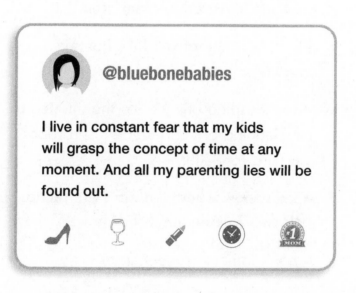

@bluebonebabies

I live in constant fear that my kids will grasp the concept of time at any moment. And all my parenting lies will be found out.

Being a mom means that it takes longer to get everyone out of the house and into the car than it does to run the errand.

Things That Would Really Help Mom (Other than *More* Wine)

- A babysitter that charges $5 an hour and isn't attracted to older men

- A nanny cam that will take home movies when Mom's too tired to do it

- A self-clasping bra (or, for that matter, a self-cleaning bra ... maybe just a robot bra ... a roBRAt!).

- A kid's show where the plots are recaps of Mom's favorite adult TV shows

- A no-judgment grocery store

- A mother who doesn't compare Mom to her sister and a mother-in-law who doesn't judge everything she does

- Just, like, ten minutes of help from her husband

The best time to take up solo
world travel is when your husband
is about to retire.

. . . . .

I thought I wanted another baby ...
then my period was an hour late.

. . . . .

I'm in a mood and my boobs hurt.
Period.

. . . . .

After a lot of consideration,
I told my husband I was okay
with seeing our kids every other
weekend. He reminded me
that we're still married and
living in the same house,
so I guess it's back to every day.

Mom: My son asked me if he could go bungee jumping.

Friend: What did you say?

Mom: No.

Friend: Why?

Mom: I don't want him to go out the same way he came in.

Friend: How's that?

Mom: Broken rubber.

Irony 101:
People who say they sleep like a baby don't have a baby.

@ashleyaustrew

4: "Mom, I'm gonna be just like you when I grow up and say bad words and eat French fries two at a time."

A woman gets on a bus with her baby.
The bus driver says, "Oh boy, that's
the ugliest baby I've ever seen!"
The woman, very insulted, goes and sits down.
The guy next to her asks what's wrong.
She tells him, "That stupid driver just insulted me!"
The man says, "March up there and tell him off!
Go ahead, I'll hold that sick dog for you."

I'd give my kids my car keys before
I gave them my wine key.

. . . . .

When my first kid was born,
I let her eat only things that
were unprocessed and organic.
By the time my third kid came around,
I let him eat anything that wouldn't
send me to jail.

. . . . .

My child's biggest
milestone wasn't their
first step or first word,
it was the first time they
wiped their own butt
and the first time they
sneezed into a tissue.

I'm convinced both of my kids are part spider because of all the time they spend on the web.

. . . . .

If a mom speaks in a room with a teenager, does it even make a sound?

. . . . .

Hi. I'm a stay-at-home mom.
Can you tell me if I'm in charge of a nuthouse,
or if I belong in one?

 @TheNYAMProject

That guy at the bar who laughs at all his own jokes that go on for way too long and thinks he's way funnier than he is, but it's my 5-year-old.

. . . .

WHAT I SAY AND
WHAT THEY HEAR

. . . .

Say: "Get ready for school."
Hear: "Put your underwear on your head."

Say: "Do your homework."
Hear: "Stare off into space while carving your name into a table."

Say: "Set the table for dinner."
Hear: "Put stickers on an old calendar."

Say: "Go outside and play."
Hear: "Lie in the middle of the floor and make mouth sounds."

Say: "I love you ..."
Hear: "I'm the most annoying person in the world and I want you to tell me something mushy."

@Six_Pack_Mom

Christmas prep is like college finals week: late nights, massive carb consumption, & the panic of knowing I should have started much sooner.

Buying label fashion used to mean
I had style. Now it means
I forgot to cut the tags off my shirts.

· · · · ·

A quiet house is all I want, but when
I get it, I know there's something
I should be worried about.

@looksliketuttut

Then suddenly you're a mom declaring ownership over swept dirt on the kitchen floor yelling DON'T YOU DARE WALK THROUGH MY DIRT PILE

My husband wants us to go
on a fancy vacation.
I told him I'd settle for a
trip alone to the bathroom.

· · · · ·

I couldn't find anyone
to help me while I was
giving birth. I guess you'd
call that a midwife crisis.

Pregnancy tip:
If you want to stop eating junk,
put it where you can't reach it.
Like the floor.

Thirty days hath September,
April, June, and November.
All the rest have thirty-one.
Except the last month you're pregnant.
That one has 12,453,308,234.

They now have pregnancy tests
designed so you don't get pee
on your hand, but not being
ready to have pee all over you
is a sign you're not ready for kids.

Judging by the reaction, the act of
a woman giving birth is almost as
painful as a man stubbing his toe.

Popular Baby Names: Then and Now

THEN	_NOW_
GIRLS:	**GIRLS:**
JENNIFER	BOTANICA
ASHLEY	HAIKU
ELIZABETH	MATCHA
LISA	TEMPEH
TIFFANY	LLIHNDUH
	(pronounced
	"Linda")
BOYS:	**BOYS:**
BRADLEY	FLINT
KEVIN	GERUND
JOSH	ALLY
MATTHEW	SATCHEL
CHRISTOPHER	P'HAL
	(pronounced
	"Paul")

I know I'm tired because I just watched my child lose his toy car keys and thought: BABIES! THEY'RE JUST LIKE US!

. . . . .

I wish they'd give me the same drugs to *raise* the kid that they gave me to have it.

. . . . .

Before I had kids, I was a size 4 in pants. Now I'm size yoga.

. . . . .

I'm not convinced that Martin Scorsese didn't direct every delivery video we watched in birthing class.

The only thing that's more painful
than childbirth is the fact that,
once the kid's out, it makes you
listen to the same songs in the car
over and over again.

. . . . .

Pregnant women are superheroes ...
but the kind who can't stand on their feet
for more than fifteen minutes without
wanting to go to sleep and who cry
at cereal commercials.

. . . . .

When I say "terrible twos," I mean
my boobs after having kids.

. . . . .

Having a baby is like
having a new car ...
once *you* get one,
you see them *everywhere.*

I'm going to be an awful mom:
I like kids and I hate wine.

. . . . .

When I had my first kid,
I made sure to make friends
with a bunch of moms so I could
get their hand-me-downs.
I called them my friends with baby-fits.

 @pro_worrier_

Watching the dogs lick up the kid's food
from the floor is the closest I get to
feeling like a Disney princess

Q: How many moms does it take to screw in a lightbulb?

A: They're too tired to screw. Can you just let them sleep?

. . . . .

I won't say which of my four kids I love most, but I give extra points to the one who can carry a glass of wine across the living room to me without spilling a drop.

. . . . .

One day I'll look up from my phone and realize ... wait, what was I saying?

. . . . .

Vitamins and minerals are a good part of my baby's meal. The other part ends up on their shirt.

My bucket list before kids:

Go skydiving

See the Taj Mahal

Sail around the world

Swim with dolphins

Read every great classic book

My bucket list after kids:

Sleep until 9:00 a.m.

See one movie in the theater

Eat a meal that doesn't have
someone else's spit on it

Finish an episode of television
without falling asleep

Go one full day without
finding food in my hair

I'll never forget my son's
first words to his father:
"Where have you been for
the past sixteen years?"

· · · · ·

When I first tried online dating
after the divorce, I used a picture
of me standing next to my kids.
But then I decided they should
probably find their own dates.

· · · · ·

My husband is a stay-at-home dad,
which is great because *my* dad was more
of the stay-away-from-home variety.

· · · · ·

I thought my seven-year-old was
mature enough to feed our goldfish—
and he is. He just isn't mature
enough to know they don't eat
peanut-butter-and-jelly sandwiches.

Husband: We have to find someone to watch the children tomorrow night.

Wife: Why?

Husband: Because if we don't, someone will come and take them away.

Wife: Sounds like a problem that solves itself.

@aissalanis

No one mentioned parenthood would include so many skipped meals but zero weight loss.

@MumInBits

Turns out if you're playing hide and seek and crawl into a super king size double duvet cover and lay still, spread out like a starfish, they won't find you and you can basically live there

I can't wait until my kids stop embarrassing me. I'm even more excited for when I can start embarrassing them.

. . . . .

My son is telling everyone that I'm a helicopter parent. I found out because my new drone gets close enough that I can read his lips.

You know you aren't getting enough sleep
when you wake up to let your cat in,
break up a fight between the cat and the dog,
go back to bed, and then wake up and
realize you don't have a cat.

· · · · ·

My husband plays fantasy football, where he
pretends to run a football team. He also plays
fantasy housekeeping, where he pretends he
does chores.

· · · · ·

If your husband is a loud sleeper, a good
solution is to wear earplugs. The only risk
is that you might never take them out.

· · · · ·

I should really get rid of my wine rack.
The bottle usually doesn't make it that far.

@VodkaAndCheeze

The hardest part of parenting is parenting your own traits out of your kids

My baby has an old soul, which sucks because I'm pretty sure I paid for a brand new one.

. . . . .

All the trials and pain of childbirth disappear the moment you see your exhausted husband shake a bottle of breast milk all over himself because he forgot to put the top back on.

MOM HACKS

Chunk up the pages of the bedtime
book to make it go by faster.

. . . . .

Trade in an extra TV episode
for story time.

. . . . .

Tell the kids any food you have
that they want has alcohol in it.

. . . . .

"We already have a dog;
you just can't see it."

. . . . .

Tire your kid out by giving them
three different names.

It's natural to favor one kid over the other sometimes, but I guess it was wrong of me to ask one of my twins to help blow up balloons for the other one's birthday party.

. . . . .

I hope they never invent Twitter for toddlers. The last thing we need is for that crew to start a social-media movement. #MePoo

 @MetteAngerhofer

"It's good for him to feel like he has some control," I say to myself after caving to yet another of my 3yo's demands.

I don't let my son watch cooking shows anymore because it might give him a better vocabulary with which to tell me that he hates my cooking.

I love when my kids ask me something that they haven't checked on the internet yet, as though somehow I'm smarter than Google.

. . . . .

My toddler woke me up at 4:00 a.m. and asked me if it was Wednesday or Thursday, and I genuinely wasn't sure how to answer.

. . . . .

If I had a dollar for every time I told my kids I only had two hands, I would be able to pay a scientist to give me six more robot hands.

Why am I always stumbling over piles of shoes, but when it's time to leave the house, no one can find a single pair?

· · · · ·

Never underestimate the power of the word "snack."

· · · · ·

Motherhood is a lot like Fight Club.
You can't talk about it to anybody
(with an adult vocabulary)
and you might even lose a tooth.

· · · · ·

I asked my child what he'd do if a stranger came up to him and said he was mommy's friend. He said, "Mommy doesn't have any friends." I have to start going to book club again.

@saltymamas

My 3yo took one bite out of every hot dog bun in the house.
Causing me to exclaim, "This is why we can't have nice things in the house!"
Causing me to realize I now consider HOT DOG BUNS to be "nice things."

Every time my toddler barges in on me in the bathroom, I get excited thinking about how much I'm going to do it to her when she's a teenager.

. . . . .

My kid just found their artwork I tried throwing away. Send help.

One of the most optimistic purchases I made
as a mother was a dresser. I don't remember
the last time any of my family's clothes
weren't in a pile.

. . . . .

I rubbed a dryer sheet on my kid's shirt
and sent him out the door to school,
so thanks but no thanks, mom who shared
her daily chore spreadsheet.

~~~~~~~~~~~~~~~~

Daylight savings:
as if moms needed one more reason to drink.

~~~~~~~~~~~~~~~~

Sometimes I can't believe I have enough
energy to pack all the loose gift bags
in my house into the biggest gift bag.

Things You Wish You Could Say to Your Teenager

"If I thought you were going to be like this, I would have sent you back when you turned twelve."

"I'm proud of you for being such a responsible driver."

"I read your diary and, quite frankly, I wish it was a little more exciting."

"We'll never talk about why I found a used condom in your coat pocket. Ever. Not even on my deathbed."

I'm probably going to go poor trying
to give my kids a rich life.

. . . . .

Every day with kids brings not only
new surprises but also a new list of things
they absolutely will not eat.

. . . . .

Slime in the Remote: A Horror Story.

We put a lot of thought into the decor
of our house. We were going to go
with midcentury but settled on
"toy store hit by hurricane."

@momtribevibe

Welcome to parenting, your choices are:
A) Listen to your toddler scream and cry for 10 minutes because YOU opened their fruit snack.
B) Listen to your toddler scream and cry for 10 minutes because THEY don't know how to open their fruit snack.

My kid asked me to lay with him
until he fell asleep.
See you in fifteen years.

. . . . .

The easiest way to clean a messy house
is to pour yourself a glass of wine
and say you'll do it tomorrow.

Marie Kondo: Does it bring you joy?

Me: (watches toddler dump grape juice on the new carpet) No.

· · · · ·

The book *What to Expect When You're Expecting* didn't help me *expect* to find an entire wall full of my son's boogers.

· · · · ·

Are toddlers weird?
Well, today we made a new
"don't put the cat's tail in your mouth" rule.
Does that answer your question?

· · · · ·

The day my kids find the
"hidden snack drawer"
is the day I move out.

I ate really well while I was pregnant with my daughter. So, I figure her eating only fruit snacks for nine months will balance out.

 @kaL12578

The gym we go to has childcare for up to 90 minutes.
Dropping my kids off: BYE BABES LOVE YOU!
Them: Have a nice workout mom!!
Me: *showers for 90 minutes*

It should be more illegal to give kids maple syrup than drugs or alcohol.

How to Work Out
If You Have a Child

STRETCH
- Reach to redo your bra clasp that your baby somehow undid in the middle of the grocery store
- Extend to find the bottle that rolled under the driver's seat

CARDIO
- Spring after your two-year-old before they walk on the carpet with muddy shoes
- Dash to the hot stove before the toddler puts their hand on it

LEGS
- Lunge to catch priceless heirlooms your kids are knocking over
- High-knee kicks walking through the living room to avoid stepping on toys

ABS
- Low plank while looking under the couch for your keys
- Crunch while rocking in pain after stubbing your toe on a toy

ARMS
- Bicep curl while grabbing two bottles of well-deserved wine. Gotta stay hydrated!

Having kids means that I have
so much more love in my life.
It also means I have more
stains on my furniture.

. . . . .

My son told me that if he had any
superpower it would be invisibility.
I couldn't agree with him more.

. . . . .

We just bought our kids a drone.
Wait, scratch that. We bought our kids
a $200 backyard tree ornament.

. . . . .

I became a songwriter after my kids were born.
The songs are mostly about convincing
someone to pee and go to bed, but I think
there's a market for that.

I'm positive that the number of times
I've told my kids "mm-hmm" while
nodding my head is going
to be my downfall.

. . . . .

Asking my kid what he wants
for lunch is really asking him which
of the five things he eats will he
throw on the ground today.

Which one's
my favorite?
Easy.
The dog.

@whinecheezits

My daughter just asked me if my boobs were ever round. In case you're wondering about some of the ways motherhood crushes your soul.

Most of the time when I hear one of my kids say, "Don't tell mommy!" I'm truly hoping they don't.

· · · · ·

Helping with homework: I guess I'm failing sixth grade math for the *second* time.

· · · · ·

Q: What do irresponsible moms and responsible bartenders have in common?

A: Neither gives shots to babies.

The worst thing you can tell your child
is that you've already seen something
they want to show you.

. . . . .

The hardest thing a mother will ever do
is not laugh when her toddler swears.

. . . . .

Nothing you did today is as impressive
as me getting my three-year-old
into a jacket and shoes in under
forty-five minutes.

. . . . .

I've potty trained a toddler
who sleeps in footie pajamas ...
I'm not afraid of hell.

@behindyourback

the most interesting thing about being the mom of a 6-year-old is knowing that I'm way too old to be cast as the mom of a teenager in any primetime tv show

Finding a Sharpie cap with no Sharpie.
Why, what's *your* worst nightmare?

. . . . .

I'd make fun of the way your baby eats,
but I actually think pigs are cute.

I should have taken the red pill
my OB-GYN offered me ...
now I'm in the MOMTRIX.

. . . . .

I had three kids, but then my youngest
compared me to *my* mother.

. . . . .

Sure, it was fun to be able to go
to live concerts on weekends and
stay out until sunrise. But it's
also fun to be woken up at sunrise on
a Saturday and listen to "Baby Shark"
for seventeen straight hours.

. . . . .

I think I have so many
overdue library books
that it's considered a felony.

Articles for Honest Women's Magazines

• • • • • • • • •

- 800 Ways You Know You're Too Tired for Sex

- Call Me when Coconut Oil Can Save My Marriage and Put My Kid through College

- How to Keep Arguing Once You've Realized You're Wrong

- Crystals and Other Mystical Choking Hazards

- It's OK to Spy on Your Kid's Teachers on Instagram: Here's Why

- Hottest Spring Dresses to Stain Beyond Repair before Leaving the House

- Best Power Foods to Eat over the Sink in a Hurry

- Sexy Swimsuits Even Your Child's Dolls Couldn't Fit Into

A fun part of my day is hiding
from my kids to eat candy.

. . . . .

I had kids because it was boring
having just my dog watch me
eat all the time.

. . . . .

The only adult show on my
"Recently Watched" Netflix list
is the stuff my kid keeps
turning on by accident.

. . . . .

I've said "mind your own business"
out loud to Netflix asking if
I'm "still watching" more times
than I'm comfortable admitting.

@milliondollrfam

Before I had children of my own, I always wondered how a parent could just ignore their kid when they're trying to talk to them.
Just want to say that I get it now.

My Friday nights are spent arguing
for two hours about which movie
I want to fall asleep to twelve minutes in.

. . . . .

I'm madder at my son for spoiling
an episode of a show I wanted to watch
than I am about him watching stuff
he shouldn't see.

By the seventh tooth, the tooth fairy
just started leaving coupons.

· · · · ·

I think I'm overloaded, but my list of chores
doesn't compare to what my kids claim
they have to get done after I tell them it's
time for bed.

 @storiesofamom

Me to child in the toy aisle:
"you do not have to touch EVERY single
toy in this store. STOP TOUCHING
EVERYTHING."
Also, me, in Homegoods:
*touches every blanket and pillow in the
blanket and pillow aisles*

Me: I can't have mac and cheese, it's all carbs and fat.

Also me: (shoving mac and cheese down my kid's throat) EAT IT!

. . . . .

I just got fired from my job, but it's okay.
I was a stay-at-home mom.

. . . . .

We have a game in my house called
"rub Mom's back for cash."

. . . . .

Pro tip:
Don't waste money on fancy diets and cleanses—
just send your kid to preschool to bring home a
stomach flu.

Mom Notes

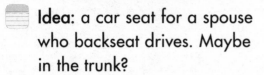

Idea: a car seat for a spouse who backseat drives. Maybe in the trunk?

Remember to pick somebody up from something sometime today

232-555-4858 is booger kid's mom's cell number

Date night is next Tuesday, so call Mom and remind her how she begged for grandkids

Google "finsta"

Shopping list: disinfectant wipes, antibacterial soap, sanitizer, hazmat uniform, a new house

Link to an article about a low-carb diet from five years ago

Remember that dream you had about the baby giraffe and your kid's teacher?

Find a recipe for whatever the hell Harper will eat for dinner

TRISH is the name of your brother's wife ... TRISHA is the name of his ex-girlfriend

A;wao4 w34tlkajlkdjfslkdjflkdjlskfj BILLY

My kids count down the numbers
to the next episode of a TV show starting
the way other people count down to
the ball dropping on New Year's Eve.

· · · · ·

People who think toddlers are cute
have never been in the middle of
potty training.

· · · · ·

That moment in a movie where someone
slides under a giant closing door is nothing
compared to getting your kid on the
school bus just before it leaves.

· · · · ·

Most of the words of encouragement I give
my kids are just slogans from commercials
from the 1980s and '90s.

@thevaginadiary

Motherhood fills your life with such joy and at the same time makes it so dull that you now look forward to things like having a Diet Coke.

We limit our kid's screen time to thirty minutes a day, or to however long it takes for me to get the longest possible nap in the middle of the day.

· · · · ·

Yoga was ruined for me when downward dog became my official butt-wiping stance.

I can tell by 5:00 a.m. if it's going to be the worst day of my life.

. . . . .

"Is it worth getting up for?"— me, when I hear something loud.

. . . . .

I decided to stop cooking for my daughter the day she told me the food I make tastes like her plastic toy food.

. . . . .

My three-year-old asked if I wanted to play "jail" with him. He doesn't seem to understand that's the game we've been playing for three years and nine months.

When my daughter was a baby, I was so
worried about leaving her with a sitter.
Now that she's a toddler, I'm always on
the verge of just throwing a helmet on her
so I can go to a movie alone.

. . . . .

My son just came home from school
with a recorder. I'm sure he'll be fine
without me for six months.

. . . . .

I thought our house was haunted.
Then I realized my toddler figured out
how to get out of his room at night.
This is scarier.

. . . . .

My four-year-old told me that
I'm "the worst mom in the world."
But he said I was the best
fifteen minutes ago,
so I figure it cancels it out.

Hot Terms Turned Blah

"MILF" is when I make a typo
on my shopping list.

"Netflix and chill" now means
fourteen hours of *PAW Patrol* while
spoon-feeding the child fever
medicine.

"DTF" now means "don't throw food."

420 is the time I have to pick up
my kid from school.

"NIFOC" just means the baby is
playing with the keyboard.

Every day is Christmas if you order stuff
from Amazon as often as I do.

. . . . .

I honestly can't tell if my kids are arguing or
having a scream conversation about cartoons.

@dishs_up

I just referred to the living room TV, our
largest, nicest, smartest TV as "your tv"
to my toddler.
If you were wondering who runs this
house.

I get so upset when my kids whine about things I think are stupid, but I just spent twenty minutes hating life because I couldn't find the ketchup I like.

If your kid tells you they didn't break something, the rest of the day is spent looking for whatever it is they broke.

. . . . .

Before I had kids, I had no way of knowing how I screwed up dinner.

. . . . .

The lightbulb was a good invention, but it's nothing compared to the strings that attach mittens to each other.

Nothing I did when I was young was
as risky as cutting my toddler's sandwich
before I asked what shape they wanted.

~~~~~~~~~~~~~~~~~~~~~~

Pro tip: Tell your kids to add whatever it is
they want during the other eleven months
to their Christmas list, too!

~~~~~~~~~~~~~~~~~~~~~~

The most impressed I've ever been
with my son is when he told me
he guessed all the answers
to a test he got an A on.

. . . . . .

Being a mom is all about
making compromises.
Like if my daughter doesn't want
to eat fruit, then she has to
share her candy with me.

Kid: What's that?

Me: A landline telephone.

Kid: What kind of apps does it have?

Me: ... you can twirl the cord.

. . . . .

I don't relate to any person more than I relate to my phone when it goes into low-power mode.

There is no slower time of day than the last half hour before my kid's bedtime.

It was a big deal when my son said his first words. But was it a bigger deal than when he learned how to use the TV on his own? Not sure.

Diaper Bag Contents

**Bottle (for baby—
previously pumped)**

**Bottle (for Mom—
wine of choice)**

Pacifier

Wipes

**TV remote you've been looking
for since four months ago**

Mystery gunk

Burp rag

Diaper cream

Protein bar covered in lint

**Old mandarin orange, or
maybe a small ball?**

Burner phone ... just in case

My son is running around an awful
lot for someone who was "too wiped"
to put his plate in the dishwasher
three minutes ago.

. . . . .

Glad I got all those new dishes for my
daughter's stuffed animals ... she just told
me they use them for toilets and, honestly,
I'm kind of proud.

@LizerReal

Parenthood: When the sound of
uncontrollable sobbing during dinner
isn't only your own.

Q: How did the Virgin Mary know she was about to give birth?

A: Her wine broke!

. . . . .

"Ride or die" as a parent refers to
driving your kids to practice and
what they say will happen to them
if you don't.

. . . . .

I don't think my kids ever love me as much
as they do when I'm late and trying to
leave the house.

. . . . .

I wish there was a snooze button
for your kid waking you up saying,
"I'm going to throw up!"

Buying new furniture for my kids
to cover up with all their junk!

. . . . .

My four-year-old just told me she wants
to be a mom someday. Clearly, she doesn't
have a handle on what she's like to live with.

. . . . .

My daughter said she wanted to know
what it was like to be married. Unfortunately,
she's too young to drink wine.

Mom's Back-to-School Shopping List

1. Bubble bath

2. Vodka

3. Vermouth

4. Olives

5. Pay-per-view "adult" movies

6. Chocolate edibles

7. Locksmith

Being a mom is needing your kids
just as much as you need them
to leave you alone.

· · · · ·

It takes my daughter longer to pick out
an outfit than it took me to decide
whether or not I wanted to have children.

· · · · ·

My four-year-old called me an idiot
while she was wearing her shoes on
the wrong feet.

· · · · ·

The real game of hide-and-seek is
seeing how long it takes for your kid
to realize you're not looking for them.

I do everything for my kids, and my kids tell me I do everything wrong.

. . . . .

I broke a mirror and my daughter said, "That's seven years of bad luck!" I didn't have the heart to tell her that—as a parent— I'm already clocked in for eighteen years of it.

 @MotherOctopusKJ

Does telling your kids that their Elf on the Shelf went out for a pack of smokes and never came back make you a bad mom? Asking for a friend.

I still get a lot of R&R as a mom:
Ranting and Raving.

· · · · ·

I could be dead, and my kid would still
ask me if they could "look at my phone."

· · · · ·

Wednesday morning before school,
my son asked if we could
"have Saturday again," and now
I think he could be president.

· · · · ·

My kids decide whether or not they hate
the food I buy for them based on how
much money I've already spent on it.

My son said he wants to be a detective when he grows up. It took him eight years to notice that our house was green.

. . . . .

The easiest way to get assassinated is by holding up the carpool lane at school.

. . . . .

It's Monday and my kids just decided they hate cheese quesadillas. So I guess they won't be getting dinner for the next week.

I want my kid to be a smart, independent thinker who always speaks their mind to everyone, but just talks to me about fun stuff.

@ramblinma

Mom friend: "Nutrition is so important."
Me, knowing full well my kids survive on
various forms of fried potatoes: "Totally."

I've never been more in favor of
education reform than I was the day
my daughter told me she'd be
learning the recorder in music class.

. . . . .

I'm going to become an Uber driver
because if I'm going to clean barf out of
my car, I'd at least like to get paid for it.

Great Ways to Announce Your Pregnancy

Wrap your positive test in a pretty box

Ultrasound picture on a "#1 GRANDPARENT" mug

Have one of your older children reveal the news

Not-So-Great Ways to Announce Your Pregnancy

Buy (or borrow) a stork

Coworker blurts it out during a budget meeting

During an intervention

At your sister's wedding ... during your matron-of-honor speech

In divorce court

At the kid's fifth birthday

With a skywriting Groupon

Have the father tell your husband

If you have kids *and* nail polish in the
same house, you're either an idiot
or you have nothing left to lose.

. . . . .

I could take my kids to a theme park …
or I could throw $1,200 in a garbage can
and light it on fire.

. . . . .

"I'm not your maid," I yelled. Then I thought
about how maids get paid to do everything
I do for free and then get to leave.

. . . . .

I trust my husband to drive our children
to school, but I don't trust him to
make my coffee in the morning.

What I say: No.

What their grandma hears: One million percent yes.

. . . . .

I never really wanted kids
until one day I thought,
"Boy, I wish I were constantly sick."

. . . . .

My son just got his driver's license.
My new favorite hobby is having him
drive me around while I scream
and kick the back of his seat.

. . . . .

My toddler is in the other room
doing something. I don't know what,
but at least he's in the other room.

The biggest win I'll have in a year is calling dibs on bringing plates and napkins to a party.

@2questionable

Parenting is basically just walking around your house picking up dirty socks and threatening to take away everything your kid loves.

"Taking a break from social media to spend more time with my family" is code for "I've been taken hostage! Please send help!"

It was my kid's first day of school today and I didn't post a picture of them on social media. Am I still a mom?

. . . . .

I'd have gone so much further in life if I'd attacked anything as intensely as my son attacks a Slip 'N Slide.

. . . . .

My daughter told me that I never let her do anything fun, and said it while she had ice cream in her mouth. Can I make a citizen's arrest?

. . . . .

My husband and I communicate more through our two-year-old telling us what the other said than we do face-to-face.

@JessicaValenti

The worst thing about being a parent is pretending I don't think homework is a scam

Watching my four-year-old son pour orange juice is more suspenseful than any movie I've ever seen.

. . . . .

I wanted kids because no one else in my life would be brave enough to scream at me that I have a pimple on my face in the middle of the mall.

I didn't understand why they
were called "throw" pillows
until I had kids.

. . . . .

Remember how you felt when your kid
said "Mama" for the first time? Well,
three years later they'll say something
like, "Mama, I pooped in the closet!"
From here on out, maybe stop listening
after "Mama."

. . . . .

You may see a giant dent in a stove.
I see a badge of motherhood.

. . . . .

My two-year-old knocked my glass of wine
onto the rug and I cried for the rug, but
mostly I cried for my wine.

Ways that Having a Dog Is Better than Having a Kid

You can leave a dog in a crate
without going to jail.

The dog is supposed to eat
on the floor.

A dog is much more likely to
listen to you when you talk to them.

Chewing shoes > chewing nipples.

You can shove the dog off the bed
if they're taking up too much space.

Paws can't throw.

You'll still get hit on—in fact,
maybe even more often.

Dogs are easier to travel with.
There's no such thing as an
"emotional support baby."

They say you can either have kids or nice things,
but not both. I think I picked wrong.

· · · · ·

My two-year-old got ahold of the remote
for literally one second, and now everything
is in hieroglyphs.

· ·

**Kids dance like nobody's watching,
but they also tell you to watch them
like nobody's watching.**

· ·

Parental perk you didn't ask for:
a free collection of children's teeth!

@MacgyveringM22

I never thought I'd be the type of mom who wakes up at 5am just so I can get a workout in before my kids get up. I was totally right.

I've been looking into getting a bigger car. Not because I want more kids, but because I want more space from the ones I already have.

· · · · ·

When my kids are fighting, if you listen very carefully, you can hear the sound of me opening a bottle of wine.

Bringing a book on a trip is like
bringing a chair to the beach: nice idea,
but probably not gonna happen.

· · · · ·

I spent $10 on a birthday card for a five-year-old.
I hate myself.

 @MissHavisham

Dentist: So, you brush, floss AND use
fluoride rinse every day?
8: Yes.
Dentist: Great!
8: Mom told me she'd buy me a Coke
Slurpee after my appointment if I said
that.
*me: already trying to climb out window

Family vacation means planning an entire day of activities, and then your kids only wanting to go back to the hotel to swim.

There are two kinds of moms:
those who go look for their kids the moment
it becomes quiet, and those who open a bottle
of wine and enjoy the break.

. . . . .

I need my kids to play sports so I'm not the only
one who yells at them.

. . . . .

Five-year-old at 5:30 a.m. on a Sunday:
What are we doing today?

Me: No.

@lifeattiffanys

5: *playing quietly*
Me: Oh no sweetie, Daddy is still sleeping. How about you go play the drums?

Trips to the beach are just a fun change of scenery for your kid's meltdown.

. . . . .

I went and did an escape room while my kids were at school, just to feel what it's like to escape something, anything.

Q: What's the difference between me when I'm nine months pregnant and a supermodel?

A: Nothing, because my husband values his life.

. . . . .

I love yelling at my kids for the things
I used to get yelled at for.

. . . . .

Turns out if I ever want my kids to not recognize me, all I have to do is put on makeup and pants with a zipper.

. . . . .

My family asks what I want for Mother's Day as I stare at a bottle of wine and a living room full of their garbage.

Notes I've Put in My Kid's Lunch Bag

I hope you like veal! It's like if someone made food out of you!

Everything in this bag can be traded for better food.

If anyone asks, tell them it's gluten free and organic.

I hope you enjoy these leftovers because we're having them for dinner too.

Make sure you say thank you to the lunch lady. Here's five bucks.

They call me a *step*parent
because I've apparently
stepped right in it.

. . . . .

I was able to get my husband
interested in our kids again by substituting
their names for cuts of steak.

. . . . .

"Silent Night" is my favorite
Christmas song and the only
thing I want this year.

. . . . .

Any game you play with your kid
could be called Risk.

@thebabylady7

Approaching the first day of school like:
please don't act like you do at home...
please don't act like you do at home...
please don't act like you do at home...

It takes a village
to raise a child,
and four grandparents
to undo all the work.

. . . . .

Look, guys.
Anything can be dinner
if I don't know about it.

Thank god for cauliflower-crust pizza …
now pizza can be a vegetable!

· · · · ·

When someone tells me that my child is
an angel, I have to ask them if they ever
went to church. As far as I know, angels
have never acted like this.

 @AcciSuperMom

Nicknaming your children is so weird.
You start off with something sweet like
Snuggle Dumpling, and before you know
it, you're calling your kid Snug Dump.

@andwhatamom

"Motherhood is a gift"
-Me, whispering to myself as I scrub dried up poop off my grandma's antique chair

Every family outing I know of is a great way to spend a lot of money watching your six-year-old grab whatever is near him and hit something else with it.

. . . . . .

My mom used to tell me only boring people are bored, but after having kids, I realize I'm never bored and I'm also never exciting. Explain that to me, Mom!

Show me something more fun than getting my kids up for school in the morning and I'll go do that ... and you can come do this.

. . . . .

My son can't pull the car out of the garage without denting it. Having been a part of his birth, I can relate to the car.

. . . . .

I love my baby so much that I cried looking at her today. I'm also going to cry when my husband comes home, and I get to go anywhere else.

. . . . .

Sure, they can make self-driving cars, but will those cars threaten to turn themselves around when my kids misbehave?

Your Baby ...

Your baby's so chubby ...
it brought a spoon to the Super Bowl.

Your baby's so bald ...
if you rub its head, you can see the future.

Your baby's so dirty ...
I bet it has to creep up on the bathwater.

Your baby's so clueless ...
your doctor had to deliver via F-section.

Your baby's so precious ...
it's being protected by sneaky little hobbits.

Your baby's so funny ...
was there an open mic in your uterus?

Your baby's so big ...
I thought you were swaddling the paper boy.

Your baby's so tiny ...
you could use a penny for a swing set.

Your baby's so scary ...
they might move Halloween to her birthday.

Your baby's so new ...
it's looks like you haven't taken the screen protector off.

Your baby's belly is so big ...
his belly button makes an echo.

Your baby's so loud ...
I bet you wore earplugs in your last trimester.

My Baby ...

My baby's like *Breaking Bad* ...
I spend a lot of time trying to get
other people to watch him.

My baby's like a new iPhone ...
I'm terrified I'm going to drop her.

My baby's like a rainy day ...
if I don't prepare myself while changing him,
I'm definitely going to get damp.

My baby's like a Journey cover band ...
when she starts up, half the people in
the room leave.

My kid's like a Tesla ...
he tries to drive everything himself
and I'm like, "I don't really trust you,
so I'm taking the wheel."

My kid's like a heated pool ...
way more expensive than any of
the fun is probably worth.

I hate being condescended to by my three-year-old. It's infuriating to be talked down to by someone I have to look down at.

Combining wine and dinner always adds up to *winner*!

. . . . .

I told my kid if he criticizes his lunch again, he'll have to make it himself. I'm planning on making liverwurst-and-banana sandwiches to speed up the process.

. . . . .

I may be a wine-drunk, single woman, but in the morning I'll wake up semi-sober (at 5:00 a.m. by a child) and you'll still be asleep (until 2:00 p.m.).

"Netflix and chill" wasn't supposed to describe your kids watching TV while their dinners get cold.

. . . . .

Homeschooling is going well, but I'm concerned one of my students will notice my coffee cup doesn't actually have coffee in it.

 @TragicAllyHere

If a person without kids says they are tired, but no parents are around to say "ha you have no idea," does it make a sound?

Me: Slow down! It's not a competition!

Me, ten minutes later: First one to fall asleep wins!

. . . . .

Just heard the kids laugh
uproariously at one of their
dad's jokes. Now I'm afraid none
of them got my sense of humor.

. . . . .

My mom voice is so good,
our dog just brushed his teeth
and went to bed too.

. . . . .

It's a difficult adjustment when
your kids move out and the
only scared side-eye you get
is from the dog.

@MotherPlaylist

My husband and I shouted at the kids to go back to bed at the same time and that's the closest we've come to a date night in weeks.

I always tell my kids that anything worth doing is worth doing *well* ... and their response is, "*Well* ... we don't *want* to."

· · · · · ·

Moms who sew all your kids' clothes: who hurt you?

I haven't gotten an appropriate amount of sleep
since 2015 BC (before children).

. . . . .

When my children ask me which one
of them is my favorite, I say it'll be the one
who lives their whole life as a productive
and considerate citizen. There, is all my
parenting done now?

. . . . .

In our family, for Mother's Day,
my husband takes the kids for the day ...
and on Father's Day, he does the same.

. . . . .

I'm nervous for the day I'm going to have to tell
my little ones that my real name isn't Mom.

. . . . .

If your husband suggests that you get a minivan,
suggest first that he gets a vasectomy.

My kid loves to go to the doctor
because she gets a lollipop,
so I told her an apple a day
keeps the dentist away to
balance it out.

Dear board game companies,

"Fun for the whole family"
isn't a real thing.

Love,
A mom

The reason a lot of moms like to drink is that,
before they were trying to conceive,
they had to drink at every meal to prove
to their mothers that they *weren't* pregnant.

Once your kids get to a certain age, their
birthday becomes less about how old *they* are,
and more about how old *you* are.

Your baby is so gross ... I bet you take him to work with you every day so you don't have to kiss him goodbye.

. . . . .

The reason I stopped wearing eye makeup after I had kids is because they don't seem to care if I get my cat eye just right.

. . . . .

They say you should try and sleep while your baby sleeps, but so far, I've only been successful at waking up whenever my baby wakes up.

. . . . .

Whenever I have the time to get my hair done, I just ask for the "please get the peanut butter out."

The sound of my baby crying is upsetting, but even more upsetting is the sound of my husband's snoring drowning her out.

. . . . .

My single friend's New Year's resolution is to go on a seven-day juice cleanse. I was interested until I found out wine doesn't count as "juice."

. . . . .

Whatever it is that makes kids start caring about being embarrassing in public … can we figure out a way to make that happen sooner?

. . . . .

My mother-in-law used to smoke around her kids, which is something I remind her of every time she says anything to me about how I raise mine.

@WalkingOutside

If you are leaving the house on time with kids fully clothed and everyone's teeth brushed and hair done, you are not a parent. You are a sitcom character.

It's not that I'm incapable of normal social interaction, it's just that I'm feeling weirded out hearing a human talk about anything other than poop.

. . . . .

I told my husband he should thoroughly discuss any advice he has on breast-feeding with his mother before telling it to me. That's how I know he's not going to have any advice.

@SparklesNSkids

Me: I wish someone would help me around here!!! Husband and kids: *fold a load of towels* Me: *refolds all the towels "the right way"*

For my birthday, my newborn got me a huge gift and even wrapped it ... in his diaper.

. . . . .

Once, in desperation, I thought I might sell my kid on eBay ... then I remembered I made him, so I should actually sell him on Etsy.

I feel the same way about seeing the bottom of the laundry hamper as I do about seeing a meteor shower or eclipse: it's rare, and fills me with awe.

. . . . .

Heck of a thing when your kid can only fall asleep while you're driving slowly down the street with soft music playing ... and the same goes for you.

. . . . .

I stopped trying to have conversations with my irresponsible friends when they complained that all I did was mad-dog them until they promised to act right.

If you've ever wrestled an armadillo in a trash bag, then you can relate to the last hour I spent getting my child out of this car seat.

Reasons to Send Your Kid to Summer Camp

1. They will finally (hopefully) make a friend

2. You'll get one of those sad, tear-stained letters that proves they actually love you

3. You can spend all your savings just to be alone for several weeks

4. Maybe their drawings will get better

5. You always need more lanyards!

6. They're going to need some context once you start letting them watch horror movies

7. They thought *your* food was bad? Welcome to a whole new level!

8. You'll have your phone all to yourself

9. Your kid *definitely* needs some new stories

10. When they come back, it's almost like you have a whole new kid!

Q: Will you love your dog less when the baby is born?

A: No, that's what husbands are for.

. . . . .

Of course it was the hockey mom who suggested that instead of arguing with one another after the game, we should go fight the baseball moms.

. . . . .

I used to love the rain. Now I see it as my archnemesis hell-bent on ruining any small amount of peace I can get.

. . . . .

Remember how they invented a new type of male birth control? Remember how we haven't heard a single thing about it since?

@MommaUnfiltered

My teenage daughter screaming "I AM BEING CALM!" just became a woman.

The toughest thing about being a mom is trying to decide which thing you do is the toughest.

· · · · ·

Mom hack: if you ever have to take care of your children *and* an elderly relative, start a game of Whining Bingo!

· · · · ·

Do we have a problem with fast food in this country? Well, it's been thirty years since I last heard a grandma say her grandkids are too skinny.

Kid: Mommy, why is everything on the floor?

Me: Ever heard of gravity? No? Well, how about children?

. . . . .

Sure, teenagers are usually quieter than toddlers, but if you had a dollar for every minute of silence, that's about how much more they cost you.

. . . . .

I try to make it a point never to judge other moms. So far, I've failed miserably.

. . . . .

Hey parents who let other people's kids drink at their house so they don't drink and drive ... what about me when I have to pick them up?!

Your baby's so old … I'm pretty sure she should have graduated from college by now. But no? Two more years? Huh. Took a break? That's cool.

. . . . .

My kids couldn't believe that I still fit into my cheerleading uniform, but they *could* believe I was so far behind on the laundry that I had to try.

. . . . .

Before I got pregnant, I did some genetic testing, and it turns out my family's DNA is just as negative as they are.

. . . . .

Moms are like precious diamonds: they withstand a lot of pressure and I don't think you want to know what it took to get them here.

@hurrahforgin

Me: *scrolling through instagram*
8 yr old: Who's that person?
Me: I don't know.
8 yr old: Who's that person?
Me: I don't know.
8 yr old: What's that dog called?
Me: I don't know.
8 yr old: Why are you looking at photos of people and dogs you don't know?
Me: I don't know...

Having a birthday is like having a toddler:
both always end in "y."

· · · · ·

When you have kids, every joke starts by
looking over your shoulder.

When it comes to eating vegetables,
my kid is like a diamond: she only cares
about the cut, the color, and the carrot.

· · · · ·

I was a tiger mom with my first child,
but now I just kind of hang around and watch my
second one ... so more like a sloth mom?

@really10months

Got the side eye from the PTA president
for mentioning there should be an open
bar at next week's fundraiser.
Calm down Carol. It's not like I said we
should do shots.

Found a sippy cup that had old milk in it
and told it, "You know what? I know *exactly*
how you feel!"

. . . . .

I have three teenagers in the house,
so my current decorating scheme is very
"there appears to have been a struggle."

. . . . .

Mom hack: change the Wi-Fi password daily,
and only hand it out once you have photographic
proof of a clean room.

. . . . .

Texted my husband: "Was watching the news
and they said they found a guy wandering around
muttering about his children. Text me back when
you can, I'm worried about you!!"

I said no to the second glass of wine,
but much like my children,
it refused to listen to me.

· · · · ·

My husband asked me to tell him
every time I have an orgasm,
but I usually find it best not to disturb him
while he's at work.

· · · · ·

I love laughing with my toddler,
even though sometimes it feels like
that moment in a buddy cop movie
right after a huge explosion and
right before the unstable character
totally loses it.

· · · · ·

I want to shop at a store that's so big,
when my kid whines I can say, "Go ahead!
There's no one around to hear you!"

@wife_housy

Me after date night with Hubs: Ugh, I'm going to change into something more comfortable
*takes off going-out yoga pants, puts on staying-in yoga pants

"Sorry to talk your ear off, Kathy!
I just haven't spoken to an adult in *ages*,"
I said to my reflection in the mirror
(that I outlined with soap).

. . . . .

I asked my kid what irony is and
he said it was the opposite of wrinkly.
If he's gonna keep that up,
I might just have to keep him.

@Megatronic13

One of the hardest parts of parenting is pretending you like vegetables

You know it's over when you ask your kid
if they're lying and they say,
"I don't know, Mom ... how about you
tell me more about Santa Claus?"

• • • • •

Accidentally happened upon a group of
moms who are apparently too good for
my secret SpaghettiOs recipe (add a
little butter), and now I gotta sneak out of
the playground like a snake-oil peddler.

They say you shouldn't put profit over people,
but I constantly have to remind my teenager
how much she's costing me.

. . . . .

Peekaboo was invented by a mom
who just needed to shut her eyes
for one moment.

. . . . .

I love my mother-in-law because she's honest.
She recently said, "I'm pretty sure I'm
totally right about some things, and about
three-quarters right on the rest."

. . . . .

Instead of a swear jar I use a MOM jar.
Every time they say "mom," they owe me a dollar.
At this point, their grandkids will probably
have to take on the debt.

Things You Wish You Had Put on Your Baby Shower Registry

1. Surrogate mother

2. The most expensive noise-canceling headphones

3. Unlimited overnight-nanny gift certificates

4. IOU an adult conversation from all your friends

5. An all-expenses paid trip to your favorite makeup store

6. A private tutor to catch you up on the outside, grown-up world

7. A Diaper Genie

8. The best "neck massager" on the market

9. An actual pause button for your career

10. A year's supply of VIAGRA for women

I made a coworker cry today by suggesting
that she put her child's car seat in the trunk
so we could carpool to lunch.

. . . . .

**To all the moms out there
who can do it all:**
I've got some stuff for you if you
get finished and get bored.

. . . . .

I understand why my kids hate it when
summer break is over. After all, margaritas
make for a mellow mom.

. . . . .

There was a time when I was considered
an interesting person. Now, I'm using
my finger to fish an old shoelace out of
a tiny person's mouth.

@RobynHTV

Parenting is 50% teaching your kids to share and 50% hiding the food you don't want to share with them.

I'd like to return my kid,
but it's a pretty steep reboxing fee.

· · · · ·

I didn't understand why kids watch
one another play video games until
I caught myself watching a show
where people remodel their homes.

The Mother's Day bar is so low for teens
that you should count it as a win if they just
look in your general direction.

. . . . .

I have a mom friend who makes macramé
plant holders and sells them online.
I'm fine with just having made a couple
of people.

. . . . .

It may not look like a pregnant woman
is doing much, but I assure you that
on the cellular level it looks like the floor
of the New York Stock Exchange.

"It's not there!"
is the first sign that
whatever they're looking
for is, indeed, there.

My friends without kids: You really have to take care of yourself. Go get a massage or a facial or a mud bath and just take it easy all day.

Me: Thanks, but for me, "self-care" looks more like an extra-long blink.

. . . . .

I didn't realize how many people throughout my life have annoyed me until I had to name a baby.

. . . . .

The only time my kid ate whatever I cooked was when we were connected by an umbilical cord.

. . . . .

It's been several months since I had my baby, but based on how my body looks, I'm gonna just tell everyone I'm having another.

Mom evolution:

Children: I have to be within 3 feet of them every second of the day!

Teenagers: I have to give them space *and* monitor them very closely.

Adults: I have to go live my life ... they can come to *me* if they want.

The difference between a kid and a husband is that you probably *want* to leave your *kid* with the babysitter.

. . . . .

I'm so sad that my son is moving out, but on the flip side it's almost like I have a new couch.

. . . . .

I want a clause in my day-care contract that says if my kid skips a nap, I get to skip a payment.

"But there was barely anything left!"—
What could have been my husband's
last words (but then he went to the store
for more ice cream).

. . . . .

Watching my toddler, I fondly
remembered my third trimester
and how I also refused to pick up
anything that fell on the ground.

. . . . .

I wouldn't be surprised if, by the time
my daughter gets pregnant, they have
pregnancy tests that indicate positive
or negative results with an emoji.

. . . . .

One thing my kids always say when I start
talking about work is "When's dinner ready?"

@Rica_Bee

My five year old calls getting kids meals at McDonald's "doing happy hour" so yeah I'm thinking this kid is definitely mine

Before kids, it took me twenty minutes to do my makeup. After kids, it takes negative-five minutes, because I'm simultaneously doing everything else.

· · · · ·

As a working mom, I have to say that working from home is the worst of both worlds.

"Having it all" feels the most
impossible when all you want
is for your kid to stop yelling.

· · · · ·

From an early age, we learned
certain truths from our mom.
The first being that she's never
"just grabbing a couple things"
at the store.

 @graceupongracie

Google history:
What do you wear to a pop concert
What do moms wear to a pop concert
Orthopedic inserts one day shipping

Q: My boobs, butt, and even my feet have gotten bigger since I got pregnant. Is there anything that gets smaller during pregnancy?

A: Your bladder.

. . . . .

It hurts so much more to be accidentally called your sibling's name once you've heard all your mom's complaints about them.

. . . . .

I've said "because I said so" for so long that my kids now fill in the "so" part.

. . . . .

Once the kids became teens, I got a dog just to feel affection from a living thing again.

● ● ● ● ● ● ● ● ● ● ● ●

The Best Mom Knock-Knock Joke

Knock knock!
Who's there?
To.
To who?
It's "to *whom*"!

● ● ● ● ● ● ● ● ● ● ● ●

What doesn't kill you makes you MOM-er!

· · · · ·

AT&T can't hold a candle to me:
I'm a mom, a taxi, a maid, a cook,
and a cellphone provider!

· · · · ·

I hope my son never asks my husband
how to tell a girl you like her, because
my husband still hasn't told me.

I wait until my sons' friends are around to remind him that he used to be in the same room with me when I pooped.

. . . . . .

I only read women's magazines for the hilarious articles that assume you have enough time to "layer" your blush.

. . . . . .

If my mother-in-law ever came over while I was trying to brush my kids' hair, I'm sure she would petition for custody.

. . . . . .

Let she who has never tried to take a toy out of its packaging make the first cut.

@effinghandbook

Just once, I would love to look my kid in the eyes when he gives me a picture he spent a long time coloring, and have the nerve to say, "could you make me another one...that's not what I wanted," just so he can get a sense of what it feels like to make him dinner every night.

Remember the end of *Titanic* ... when Kate Winslet's taking up the entire door? That's every night that my kid insists on sleeping in bed with me.

. . . . .

After you have kids, it seems like you should be able to add some amendments to your wedding vows.

For our anniversary, my husband and I were able to do all the same things we used to do, except with screaming kids hanging from our limbs.

. . . . .

Guarding your pooping child in a public bathroom by standing outside their stall holding a lightsaber? Yeah ... that's as cool as it sounds.

. . . . .

As we were leaving the grocery store, my niece and nephew yelled that they wanted some "Auntie Wine." Well played, Sis ... well played.

. . . . .

I always feel most alone right before I look up and see a little face in the doorway, watching me pee.

When my mom yells my name
over and over again, I know it's just
payback for what I did as a kid.

. . . . .

Do those moms who love wine
even know that vodka exists?

 @IjeomaOluo

Amtrak conductor: "Ladies & Gentlemen,
keep on your shoes. Parents, dress your
children."
This woman knows the horrors of travel

Ways to Limit
Your Kids' Screen Time

1. Speak to them on their level: "I honestly think you are, literally, like, constantly on your phone, like, hundo P. This is no open crib. It would be straight fire if you would put your phone down."

2. Send them to the Amish for a summer.

3. "Accidentally" knock their phone into a glass of water.

4. Turn off the family Wi-Fi and turn on the secret Wi-Fi they don't know about.

5. Invent an app that automatically calls their grandparents every time they try to do something on their phone.

6. Scream into the indifferent maw of the universe. It's just as effective.

@thetonihammer

6yo: Mom, can I—
Me: You can do anything you want as long as I don't have to get up.

Bikini season? Maybe for you …
I just had a baby, so I'm getting ready
for swimsuit cover-up season.

· · · · ·

When my daughter tells a really good joke,
I feel proud. When she tells a really bad one,
I know she's been talking to her dad.

Mom: I have a rule that if my kids act up, we go home, no matter where we are. That way they know misbehaving is never tolerated.

Him: That's cool, lady, but could you just sign right here? I've got other pizzas to deliver.

. . . . .

I don't know why I thought telling my mom that I'm going to get back together with my boyfriend was a good idea; she still prank calls the kid who called me "silly" in kindergarten.

. . . . .

My daughter's birth was more like takeout than delivery.

My friends think they want to hear horror stories about childbirth, but I keep telling them they're just gonna come out wrong.

MOM JOKES

It doesn't take Sherlock Holmes
to know that if Mom's eating ice cream out
of the carton when Dad gets home ...
he might want to steer clear.

. . . . .

My kids know that if they ignore me
while they're on their phones, I'm going
to destroy their Minecraft village while
they're asleep.

. . . . .

I never took the time to consider if I could
live with my husband's chewing sounds.
Now I've got four of him at the dinner table.

. . . . .

"What the hell, Mom should have had
dinner already," I thought to myself ...
and then to my horror realized Mom is me.

@eff_yeah_steph

Coffee tastes better when you use filtered water and your kids are still asleep.

My kids had to teach themselves how to cook while I was ill. Good thing, too. Turned out I was just sick of cooking for them.

• • • • • •

There's a point when you're homeschooling where it feels like maybe you should just let your kids be YouTube celebrities.

Going to bed at 10:00 p.m. would be a blessing, if only I fell asleep before 3:00 a.m.

@rachelaxler

eventually i will be my son's mother, but currently i am just a 24hr breastaurant

My friend can't come to my son's wedding because it's her cat's birthday, and now I wish I'd just gotten a cat.

I've been out of popular culture for so long that when I'm with my hip friends, I roll my eyes and say, "Yeah, but, like, ToyPudding is the new Beat Bugs ..." and it works *every* time.

. . . . .

After his thousandth bad joke, I got my husband a T-shirt that says, "Moms Are Funny and Dads Are Just Punny!" What sucks is that he loves it.

. . . . .

I like my son's new girlfriend so much that I'm starting to think it's time she had a proper boyfriend.

New rule: the parent who gets to spend the day away from the kids has to listen to the other one talk for thirty uninterrupted minutes afterwards.

Mom Haiku

Here comes the choo-choo!
Nope. Airplane? Nope. Boat? Nope. Car?
We'll drive to Grandma's.

You know you're done having kids
when the last one tells you he almost
ran out of womb in there.

· · · · ·

Some guy hit on me and my
daughter today. I think he thought
we were twins because I said
we were separated at birth.

My little brother rushed to the
hospital after learning his niece
couldn't stand or talk ...
can't believe Mom never
taught him about newborns.

. . . . .

I've decided to call my newborn baby
Destroyer of Worlds until I can think of
something more fitting.

. . . . .

If my husband were to ever bet
our child in a game of poker,
I'd definitely have to raise him.

. . . . .

My dad says he doesn't understand
kids these days, but I assured him
my kids don't understand adults
from his day either.

Grandparents love to watch their children's children misbehave, and then act all surprised when they still do it as teens.

· · · · ·

I'll take my kids on vacation with me once they prove they can all walk ten feet in the same direction without anyone screaming.

· · · · ·

You'd think I'd be more sympathetic to my teenager. After all, I know what it's like to be possessed by hormones. But then again, I really can't stand a$$holes.

· · · · ·

When all the mothers in my family get together, it's worse than a group of veterans talking about the worst things they've seen in war.

I would rather have someone look in my medicine cabinet than my recycling bin.

· · · · ·

The easiest part of my day is deciding to not get up and help my husband get the kids ready for school.

 @Elizasoul80

Ah yes, the day after mother's day. Back to not being appreciated by the tiny food terrorists in my house.

Kid: Mommy! I didn't know where you were!

Mom: That sounds like a problem that fixes itself!

· · · · ·

My kids know all about my roots,
and I've sworn them to secrecy until
I have the time to dye them again.

· · · · ·

If your husband has any interest in
staying your husband, he better not reply
"Nice!" after you get up the nerve to
send a nude pic.

· · · · ·

Don't tell my kids, but the easiest way to
distract me is to hand me a magnifying
mirror and a pair of tweezers.

@Darlainky

Me then: You kids have to stop leaving your toys everywhere!
Me now: Awww the dogs left their toys everywhere, they're so cute.

My kids act like one day their dad and I are going to turn around and announce we've been filthy rich this whole time and are just trying to teach them character.

· · · · ·

No one warns you that someday every person in your house might snore.

I spend 50 percent of my time
making sure that everyone's
gone to the bathroom.
And the other 50 percent
finding out too late that they
were all lying.

. . . . .

Fun fact: if your child is screaming in the middle
of the grocery store, you can tell people it's not
yours.

. . . . .

My fifteen-year-old communicates with me
exclusively through a language of
shoulder shrugs and eye-rolling.

. . . . .

These days the best way to punish a
twelve-year-old is to unfollow them
on Instagram.

• • • • • • • • • • • • • •

Worst Parenting Advice from Strangers

1. Use crystals (and do what with them, exactly?)

2. Let your baby cry it out (until you lose every shred of sanity)

3. Never negotiate with your kids (look, the terrorists have already won)

4. Let them pick their own name (cool, now my kid's name is Cheese Unicorn)

5. Force your kids to play sports (now I never get to sleep in)

6. Always give them a home to come home to (I don't think they're ever going to leave)

• • • • • • • • • • • • •

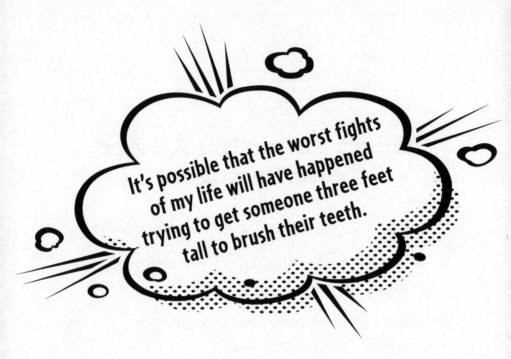

It's possible that the worst fights of my life will have happened trying to get someone three feet tall to brush their teeth.

Q: My husband wears boxers instead of briefs. That makes it easier to get pregnant, right?

A: I guess. It's probably even easier if he doesn't wear anything, though.

. . . . . .

Face masks used to be a thing I did to relax. Now they're just a way for me to scare my kids.

My kids learned how to swear in every language but refuse to learn how to say "Thanks, Mom" in this one.

. . . . .

The last time I made my kid a healthy breakfast, I got laughed at harder than I ever did in school.

. . . . .

I knew I was a mom the day my toddler coughed in my eye and I didn't blink.

@curlycomedy

Sometimes I'll throw in a food with my baby talk like "little cookie baby" or "special little pancake," and realize it's because I'm hungry.

I love bringing my kids to
the amusement park.*

*The escalator at any department store

· · · · ·

Every year I get my kids the nicest
gifts for their birthdays. They usually
get me sick for mine.

 @outsmartedmommy

No one told me that part of motherhood
is pretend laughing at knock knock jokes
about butts. A warning would have been
nice.

The abbreviation "SAHM" caught on because stay-at-home moms didn't have enough time or energy to say the whole thing.

· · · · ·

I'm at that stage in my life where the least exciting thing on Earth is having someone tell you they're pregnant.

· · · · ·

My ancestors came to this country to avoid a dictator. But the way my four-year-old talks to her little sister, seems like we might have to move again.

· · · · ·

I love my kids the exact amount of the battery percentage on my phone when they give it back to me.

There are eight rings in mom hell.
Each ring signifies the number of practices
you have to take your kids to in a day.

. . . .

If parenthood were a candle, it would smell like Cheerios and regret.

. . . .

If I learned anything by sending my kid
to band camp, it's that sometimes it's
safer to invest in a pyramid scheme than
in your child's hobbies.

. . . . .

The tooth fairy's schedule is wholly
dependent on how late you made the
tooth loser go to bed.

Back to school for them, and back to filling out back-to-school forms for me!

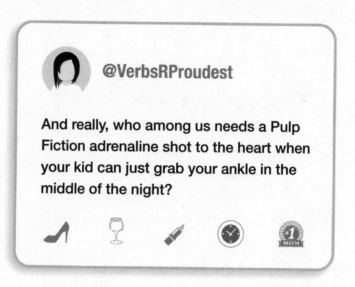

@VerbsRProudest

And really, who among us needs a Pulp Fiction adrenaline shot to the heart when your kid can just grab your ankle in the middle of the night?

Twenty years from now, my kids are going to ask where all their baby pictures are, and I'll point to a shoebox filled with my old phones.

Materials for dyeing Easter eggs:

eggs

food coloring

two kids who fight over everything

a full bottle of wine

The summer solstice is the second longest day of the year, after a day your kid won't take a nap.

@TheMudlily

Do you come here often? You look so familiar. -Stephen the target cashier to me just now.
Yes Stephen. Yes I do.

The only thing worse than having no coffee in the house is also having all the kids in the house.

· · · · ·

Finally got all the sand out of my car from the last time we all went to the beach ... which was seven years ago.

· · · · ·

All the adult shows on cable are also great for kids ... to walk in on and interrupt when we thought they were in bed.

LEGO didn't *invent* the
worst way to hurt yourself
while walking on carpet,
but they sure perfected it.

. . . . .

The word "mother" exists
because it sounds better than
"human napkin."

@MamaFizzles

My son says I only had kids so
I could make them do chores. Like yes,
I made a bunch of messy, whiny poop
machines so they could cry while doing
a crap job of cleaning that I just have
to redo later.

Friend: You look great! I can't believe you just had a baby!

New mom: Thank you. I can't tell if it's been three weeks or three years and also my eyes are so blurry, I can no longer see my own reflection in a mirror.

· · · · ·

I would rather listen to three solid days
of hold music than another minute
of any cartoon-movie soundtrack.

· · · · ·

After the last flight with our
eight-month-old son, there's no way
he isn't on everyone's "no fly" list.

· · · · ·

I thought I could run away from my problems.
But all three of them found me hiding in the shower.

@susanorlean

I love torturing my 13 yo son by telling him I plan to start wearing overalls.

If you're willing to fight with someone about whether or not the yolk of an egg is made out of cheese, you're going to love parenting.

. . . . .

Having teenage boys means finding new, amazing ways for anything around the house to be done very, very poorly.

I call the glass of wine I have before bath time the "calm before the storm."

· · · · ·

I don't remember all the things I wanted to be when I grew up, but "tired lady who always has Cheerios dust under her fingernails" wasn't one of them.

 **@GrownandFlown**

It's cute how teens think they can sneak in the door at 1AM without us noticing like we haven't been staring out the window and seething for past 182 minutes.

Leaving on time means never letting
your toddler do anything on their own
to get ready.

. . . . .

I'll get a picture of bigfoot riding a unicorn
before I'll get a picture of all my kids
standing still and smiling.

. . . . .

Had the same thing for dinner I have
every night: a screaming match between two
kids who are mad at each other for existing.

. . . . .

My greatest accomplishment as a mother
is when I'm able to keep one kid from
waking the other up.

Five Signs You're Finally Bonding with Your Stepchild

1. They've stopped referring to you as *eyeroll*.

2. They finally realized you're the one buying their dad's presents on their behalf.

3. For the first time, they played princess with you, and you didn't have to be the evil queen.

4. When you drop them off, they wave goodbye instead of waving one finger.

5. They laugh with you when someone calls them your "bonus kids" instead of at you after they call *you* "stepmonster."

@ThatEvansLady

Well, you're up early.
-Me, greeting my children every morning
since they were born

"It's been scientifically proven that the dirtiest place on Earth is the play area in a pediatrician's waiting room" isn't holding any weight with my toddler.

· · · · ·

You can't expect your kids to help clean up when you ask them to, but it's nice to know that you can get rid of them in a hurry with the mere suggestion.

I can't decide which I'd rather do a second time: go through childbirth or watch my kid try to zip himself up.

. . . . .

As a mom, you spend more time thinking and talking about your kid's poops than you do current events.

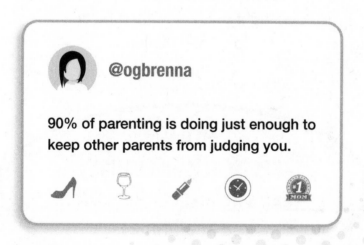

@ogbrenna

90% of parenting is doing just enough to keep other parents from judging you.

Went to the zoo with my kids.
They lost a toy, a bottle, a sock, and a hat.
I lost my mind.

. . . . .

As a mom, the one question you never stop
asking yourself is, "What is *on* this?"

. . . . .

I love playing games with my kids.
Especially the ones where I can
"die" right away and then lie down
for a few minutes.

MOMS:
KEEP CALM and CARRY
extra animal crackers ON
you at all times.

@NoSleepInBklyn

No One Listens Until I Yell: the name of my parenting memoir.

I must have told my kids over a billion trillion times not to exaggerate, but they refuse to *ever* hear a *single* word I say.

. . . . .

A big part of being a mother is learning how to pretend like you've got it all figured out.

Nothing is really lost until Mom can't find it,
but then discovers it wedged behind the dryer
twenty years later.

· · · · ·

A fun thing to do is to whisper-scream *"Get out!"*
to any woman who looks at your family and says
she can't wait to have kids, too.

@misslillytoyou

2yo is passed out, clutching a fist full of
fries. She's 100% mine.

The greatest trick the devil ever played was allowing the kids to stay up an extra hour when he's the one who gets to sleep in the next morning.

. . . . .

My mom types like she had a plastic surgeon swap her fingers and toes.

. . . . .

Do they give you something if your kid screams during the whole plane ride? No, not like a medal. More like a Valium?

. . . . .

#JustFoundOutWhatAHashtagIs #PrettyCool #ThanksSon

Moms get Mother's Day, but my kid gets her birthday, Christmas, summer vacation, and Boss's Day. And most other days, depending on her mood.

@JenniferBorget

My kids won't go to sleep & they're driving me nuts. Also trying my first facemask so I'm about to scare the living daylights out of them.

It's important to be a mom first and a friend second. Unless your friend is old enough to buy you more wine.

Q: How many moms does it take to get a four-year-old to go to bed?

A: I don't know, but definitely more than one.

. . . . .

A child's laugh can be one of the
most beautiful sounds in the world,
but my kid sounds like a goblin
who just tricked someone into
giving him their firstborn.

. . . .

**A mom is a lot like a sock:
both might someday disappear
under a mountain of laundry.**

. . . .

My husband's superhero power
is to make all the kids start screaming
and running right before bedtime …
I've got to find out what his kryptonite is!

Mom 1: How's your teen doing in school?

Mom 2: Pretty well … he *loves* drama.

Mom 1: He's taking drama class?

Mom 2: No …

My child is too young to have seen *The NeverEnding Story*, but he definitely recognizes the theme song, which I start singing every time his stories go long.

· · · · ·

Me, stopping at the drive-through after work: "I'd like one free child care, please!"

My kids just found out about sarcasm,
so I'd like to return them for store
credit, please.

· · · · ·

My husband took us on a road trip
for vacation. Turns out at the end of it
I needed a vacation because of the vacation.

 @closetoclassy

You're not living your best parenting life
until you've launched a toy out the front
door to stop your kids from fighting
over it.

@marriagemartini

My kids throw a lot of shade for tiny people completely dependent on me for survival.

I became a mom the day my son rolled his eyes at me for the first time.

. . . . .

It's very important to me that my family sits down at the table every night and has a civilized dinner, and that's only possible if I cook with CBD oil.

What a moment it is when your kid says,
"But every day is Mother's Day, Mommy!"
And then the next day, they scream for
five hours straight.

· · · · ·

The most precious thing I've ever had
around my neck are the arms of my
children, and I blame my husband for
every aspect of that.

· · · · ·

My son asked why I came home so early
from work. I explained that my boss told me
to go to hell.

· · · · ·

Started a garden so my kids would eat
more greens. I may as well have planted
jelly beans and green M&M's.

Money isn't everything,
but don't tell my kids that.
It's the only reason they call.

. . . . .

As a mom, you have to look out
for number one. Otherwise your
baby will pee all over you.

. . . . .

One of the biggest mistakes of
being a mom is thinking
that if your kid is active during
the day, they'll go to bed early and
sleep through the night like a person.

. . . . .

White wine goes with fish and
red wine goes with steak,
but either goes with rotten children.

It just occurred to me that if my daughter becomes a famous artist, I've already thrown out maybe a million dollars' worth of her work.

• • • • •

Every Thanksgiving I make dinner for my entire extended family, because I'm the only one who has Stockholm syndrome.

@valeegrrl

Hey, parents of an only child considering having one more, know that I just split an M&M in half.
An M&M.
In half.

@BPMbadassmama

Don't be so hard on yourself. The mom in E.T. had an alien life form living in her house for days and she never even noticed.

I drink eight glasses of water a day. Well, all wine was water before Jesus got ahold of it, right? Doesn't that count?

· · · · ·

I walked in on my husband bent over cleaning up a spill. He turned to me and asked if I saw anything I liked. I said, "Yeah, Baby … you doing housework."

The only vacations that count are
the ones that start with you
taking your kids to your parents' house.

. . . . .

I'm finally getting through to my teen.
I only had to ask him to set the table 439 times.
Yesterday it was 440.

. . . . .

I asked my mother-in-law if she
would give me her secret recipe
for the cookies my husband loves,
and she emailed me this:

$$(x + a)^n = \sum_{k=0}^{n} \binom{n}{k} x^k a^{n-k}$$

If you only do missionary position,
does that mean you're in
a same-sex marriage?

. . . . .

My daughter saw my search history,
so now I have to come up with
a backstory for why I googled
"How do I start a new life?"

 @paigekellerman

In the dictionary, the definition of
"tedious" just has a picture of a toddler
trying to open a Capri Sun by himself.

Give a man a task and
he'll resent you for a day.
Give a man a list and
he'll probably start looking
for a second family.

· · · · ·

Before asking a stranger if she's pregnant,
ask yourself if you're feeling lucky.
Well? Are you, punk?

· · · · ·

It seems like it was only yesterday that I was
waiting for my daughter to pick out an outfit
for her doll. Oh wait, it was yesterday ...
I fell asleep. She still hasn't picked out an outfit.
Going back to sleep.

· · · · ·

Once a month I have to apologize
to my partner for ovary-acting
to some dumb thing they do.

It's really popular to give birth in water now because it's less traumatic for the baby, although I can't say the same for the senior aqua-aerobics class at the YMCA.

. . . . .

To keep your newborn as comfortable as possible, make sure to set your nursery to womb temperature.

. . . . .

I use the same technique for my birth control as I do with my debit card: pull out and pray.

. . . . .

I call my kids so much that they think I'm the background on their phones.

Things You Never Hear a Mom Say

"Use one of the power tools for that!"

"Sure. I've got plenty of time."

"You're right ... this dinner *sucks!*"

"Come on in, I'm fully rested."

"Yeah, grab whatever you want. That's *why* we came down the candy aisle!"

"Tell me that story one more time."

"Of course you can get a goldfish. I'll never check in on it."

"They're just teeth."

"Whatever it is you're doing with your plate of uneaten food is *amazing!*"

"Well, sure! If *everybody's* doing it ..."

@3sunzzz

When I see how my boys have loaded the dishwasher I think, "Maybe their father is my cousin."

A woman I know has two kids, and they all sleep together in what she calls a "family bed," which, to me, are the last two words in the English language you should ever put together.

. . . . .

They make a bra that has a pouch you can fill up with wine. Finally, *someone* is listening to me!

Having twins is fun because we have a secret language: my husband and I invented a ton of new cuss words to use when they piss us off.

· · · · ·

My daughter just tried to convince me she was too sick to go to school. It's the first time in years that I've seen the Best Actress performance for the Oscars.

 @ericawhotoyou

You aren't a real mom until you have a car with an overstuffed glove compartment filled with napkins stolen from fast food restaurants.

Pajama Day is my favorite holiday.

· · · · ·

Title of summer vacation:
How Many Snacks Can You Possibly Eat?

· · · · ·

It's hard enough remembering what
our Wi-Fi password is, now I need a
verbal one to get into my son's room?

 @lurkathomemom

Parenting is fun if you're into things like
cooking for people who aren't hungry.

The most stressful day at my job doesn't come close to the stress of finding a two-year-old with an open permanent marker.

I want the confidence of my daughter, who called me "the worst mom ever" and then asked me to drive her to her friend's house.

. . . . .

My daughter got mad and said I don't let her have any fun. It's not my fault that her idea of fun is pinching her five-month-old brother.

@gfishandnuggets

My 5-year-old just told me that turtles are slow because they carry their houses on their backs, and I feel like this is a solid analogy for parenthood.

Getting our furniture cleaned is just like shaking an Etch A Sketch.

· · · · ·

Every time I have to re-wash a dish my husband washed the day before an angel loses its wings.

"Stepmom" isn't a bad word, but that other word you used to refer to me is.

. . . . .

My idiot husband just said, "I'm *nacho* usual dad!" and walked away and now everyone is screaming for nachos.

. . . . .

"If you thought grandmas spoil your kids, wait until you see what I've got up my sleeve!"
—Great-grandmas

My ex-husband's wife is so young that I remind him of it every single time I talk to him.

@nicfit75

I needed a pack of 49 cent index cards from Target so yeah, of course, I just spent $238.

I got a Mother's Day card from my grandmother that just said, "Wait for it … this is the life, Baby!"

. . . . . .

When rich celebrities talk about how hard parenthood is, I can't help but think I should scream into a pillow until my gums bleed.

This Christmas, I'm giving my kids only two gifts:
one thing they're going to complain about,
and the return slip.

. . . . .

My sixteen-year-old daughter asked
me what it's like to become a mom,
so I described an episiotomy in great detail
until she left the room.

@thatmummylife

I woke up with this horrible, debilitating
pain in my neck this morning and I have
no idea what's causing it.
remembers having kids
Oh.

I once dated a guy with a parrot.
The thing never shut up . . .
the parrot was cool, though.

. . . . .

Stepparenting:
if you thought parents were the enemies,
wait till you get a load
of these guys!

 @sarcasticmommy4

Welcome to parenthood. You have a
favorite closet to hide & eat your snacks
in now.

@KateWouldHaveIt

"We don't wear what we slept in out in public." —Me, lying to my child

I dated a tennis player in college.
Love meant nothing to him.

· · · · ·

For Halloween, I want to
put a fake beard on my baby
and walk around the neighborhood
breast-feeding him.

IMAGE CREDITS